JAPANESE GOVERNMENT AND POLITICS

Front Cover: Emperor Meiji in a formal session of the House of Peers. Source: Wikimedia Commons.

Back Cover: *Nobori* flags (banners) held by a group of pro-Article 9 demonstrators and their police escort near the Ginza neighborhood of Tokyo. Source Wikimedia Commons.

Key Issues in Asian Studies, No. 22

AAS Resources for Teaching About Asia

JAPANESE GOVERNMENT AND POLITICS

LAUREN MCKEE

Association for Asian Studies, Inc.
825 Victors Way, Suite 310
Ann Arbor, MI 48108 USA
www.asianstudies.org

KEY ISSUES IN ASIAN STUDIES

A series edited by Lucien Ellington, University of Tennessee at Chattanooga

"Key Issues" volumes complement the Association for Asian Studies' teaching journal, *Education About Asia*—a practical teaching resource for secondary school, college, and university instructors, as well as an invaluable source of information for students, scholars, libraries, and those who have an interest in Asia.

Formed in 1941, the Association for Asian Studies (AAS)—the largest society of its kind, with close to 6,000 members worldwide—is a scholarly, non-political, non-profit professional association open to all persons interested in Asia.

For further information, please visit www.asianstudies.org

Copyright © 2023 by the Association for Asian Studies, Inc.

Published by the Association for Asian Studies, Inc. All Rights Reserved. Written permission must be secured to use or reproduce any part of this book.

AAS books are distributed by Columbia University Press.

For orders or inquiries, please visit https://cup.columbia.edu

Library of Congress Cataloging-in-Publication Data

Names: McKee, Lauren, author.
Title: Japanese government and politics / Lauren McKee.
Description: Ann Arbor, MI : Association for Asian Studies, [2023] |
  Series: Key issues in Asian studies; Volume 22 | Includes
  bibliographical references. | Summary: "This volume takes a comparative
  approach to Japanese politics, covering topics such as political parties
  and elections, civil society, bureaucracy, and foreign relations.
  Grounded in a discussion of democracy's historical development since the
  Meiji period, each chapter encourages readers to think critically and
  comparatively about political processes and their outcomes, situating
  Japan regionally and as a wealthy, democratic nation. The goal is to
  offer students of government insight into how democracy works—and
  doesn't, for that matter—and can illustrate the fact that strengthening
  democratic institutions is an ongoing struggle throughout much of the
  world, including Japan"— Provided by publisher.
Identifiers: LCCN 2022060599 | ISBN 9781952636356 (paperback) | ISBN
  9781952636363 (ebook)
Subjects: LCSH: Political science—Study and teaching—Japan. |
  Democracy—Study and teaching—Japan. | Civil society—Study and
  teaching—Japan | Japan—Politics and government—History. |
  Japan—Foreign relations.
Classification: LCC JA88.J3 M37 2023 | DDC 320.952071—dc23/eng/20230103
LC record available at https://lccn.loc.gov/2022060599

This book is dedicated to my students,
in appreciation for all they've taught me.

About "Key Issues in Asian Studies"

Key Issues in Asian Studies (*KIAS*) volumes engage major cultural and historical themes in the Asian experience. *Key Issues* books complement the Association for Asian Studies' teaching journal, *Education About Asia*, and serve as vital educational materials that are both accessible and affordable for classroom use.

Key Issues books tackle broad subjects or major events in an introductory but compelling style appropriate for survey courses. Although authors of the series have distinguished themselves as scholars as well as teachers, the prose style employed is accessible for broad audiences. This series is intended for teachers and undergraduates at two- and four-year colleges as well as advanced high school students and secondary school teachers engaged in teaching Asian studies in a comparative framework and anyone with an interest in Asia.
For further information visit www.asianstudies.org.

Prospective authors interested in *Key Issues in Asian Studies* or *Education About Asia* are encouraged to contact Lucien Ellington, University of Tennessee at Chattanooga; Tel: (423) 425-2118; E-Mail: Lucien-Ellington@utc.edu.

"Key Issues" volumes available from AAS:
- *Shintō in the History and Culture of Japan* / Ronald S. Green
- *Indonesia: History, Heritage, Culture* / Kathleen M. Adams
- *The Philippines: From Earliest Times to the Present* / Damon L. Woods
- *Chinese Literature: An Introduction* / Ihor Pidhainy
- *The Mongol Empire in World History* / Helen Hundley
- *Japanese Literature: From Murasaki to Murakami* / Marvin Marcus
- *Japan Since 1945* / Paul E. Dunscomb
- *East Asian Societies* / W. Lawrence Neuman
- *Confucius in East Asia* / Jeffrey L. Richey
- *The Story of Việt Nam: From Prehistory to the Present* / Shelton Woods
- *Modern Chinese History* / David Kenley
- *Korea in World History* / Donald N. Clark
- *Traditional China in Asian and World History* / Tansen Sen & Victor Mair
- *Zen Past and Present* / Eric Cunningham
- *Japan and Imperialism, 1853–1945* / James L. Huffman
- *Japanese Popular Culture and Globalization* / William M. Tsutsui
- *Global India ca 100 CE: South Asia in Early World History* / Richard H. Davis
- *Caste in India* / Diane Mines
- *Understanding East Asia's Economic "Miracles"* / Zhiqun Zhu
- *Political Rights in Post-Mao China* / Merle Goldman
- *Gender, Sexuality, and Body Politics in Modern Asia* / Michael Peletz

About the Author

LAUREN MCKEE is associate professor of political science and Asian Studies at Berea College. She first joined the faculty of Berea College in 2014 as an ASIANetwork-Luce Foundation postdoctoral teaching fellow after receiving a PhD in international studies from Old Dominion University. Dr. McKee regularly works with the National Consortium for Teaching about Asia (NCTA) and has published in the Association for Asian Studies (AAS) teaching journal, *Education about Asia*. She enjoys teaching classes on comparative and East Asian politics and has taken students  on study trips to Japan and China. Dr. McKee recently joined the US-Japan Network for the Future, an initiative dedicated to promoting bilateral policymaking and US-Japan understanding, which is sponsored by the Maureen and Mike Mansfield Foundation and the Japan Center for Global Partnerships.

CONTENTS

LIST OF FIGURES

Acknowledgments

I am grateful to many people for their help in preparing this book. Rebecca Bates read early drafts and offered helpful feedback. Jeff Richey provided encouragement and support throughout the writing process. Together with Rob Foster, John Heyrman, and Mike Berheide, I could not ask for more tireless advocates at Berea College. Jeffrey Kingston offered his perspective on populism in Japan. Two anonymous reviewers offered their time to read the manuscript and provided insightful feedback. My late mentor and friend, Steve Yetiv, demonstrated how to be a productive scholar who keeps work in perspective. My husband, Martin Veillette, was patient enough to listen to countless versions of the same paragraph and always knew when my spirits needed lifting. My mother, Sheila Shoemake's, confidence in my abilities is steadfast and unconditional, even as she regularly reminds me of the going rate for an ounce of pretension. Without these people, this project would certainly have been less fun and undoubtedly less good.

An immense debt of gratitude goes to Key Issues editor Lucien Ellington. We first began this project in late 2019, unaware of the coming COVID-19 pandemic and the many ways it would change our working lives. Lucien remained patient and professional, always pushing me to meet the high standards for which the Key Issues series is known. I am a better writer for having worked with him. I am also grateful to Jon Wilson for selecting the perfect cover image and for making the publication process painless.

Finally, I am grateful to my students at Berea College for helping me think more deeply about the importance of politics in lived experiences.

Editor's Introduction

Lauren McKee's *Japanese Government and Politics* is a well-written and interesting volume that should be useful for a wide range of readers, including instructors and students who are for the most part unfamiliar with Japan or have no prior knowledge of Japanese politics or government. Potential classes where the book may be used as a supplementary reading include: introductory undergraduate survey level comparative politics courses; introductory undergraduate survey courses on modern Japan; AP and high school comparative politics courses; and potentially, high school and university introductory courses in American government. Virtually every US government textbook at the secondary school or undergraduate level includes a chapter on either comparative government or foreign policy. This book will also be useful in East Asia institutes for middle and secondary school teachers, as has been the case with several *Key Issues* volumes.

Lauren begins her Introduction with an anecdote that promises to engage readers of various ages. The first chapter is a succinct but rich contextualization of Japanese politics and government, beginning with the Asuka Period (538–710 CE) through the end of World War II. In the ensuing chapters, Lauren's narrative on Japan's bureaucracy, elections, political parties, civil society, and political participation, as well as additional chapters in the volume, is consistently well-written, includes critiques and multiple perspectives, and is well organized. It was a privilege to collaborate with Lauren on the volume, because of her receptivity to suggestions, work ethic, positive attitude, and professionalism.

As is always the case, the successful development of this volume would have been impossible without the help of several people. Robert David Eldridge read the initial proposal. Manuscript referees Dyron Dabney and Dan Métraux provided helpful constructive criticism. Jon Wilson AAS Publications Manager, the AAS Editorial Board, and especially the Chair Bill Tsutsui continually provide solid support for the AAS's pedagogical publications *Key Issues in Asian Studies* and *Education About Asia*.

The publication of Lauren's volume is especially significant for Berea College, the only institution of higher learning where two faculty members have published *Key Issues* volumes in the history of the series. Jeffery Richey recently published a second edition of his successful volume *Confucius in East Asia*. Berea faculty such as Jeff and Robert Foster built an exemplary Asian Studies program. This will be no surprise for readers who are familiar with Berea College's success in providing liberal arts education for students with limited economic resources while retaining outstanding faculty scholars *and* teachers.

Timeline

Prehistoric and Ancient Japan

Jōmon period: roughly 13,000 BCE–1,000 BCE

Yayoi period: roughly 1,000 BCE–250 CE

Kofun period: roughly 250 CE–538 CE

Classical Japan

Asuka period: 538 CE–710 CE

Nara period: 710 CE–794 CE

Heian period: 794 CE–1185 CE

Feudal Japan

Kamakura period: 1185 CE–1333 CE

Muromachi period: 1333 CE–1568 CE

Sengoku "Warring States" period: 1467 CE–1615 CE

Azuchi-Momoyama period: 1568 CE–1600 CE

Edo or Tokugawa period: 1600 CE–1868 CE (early modern Japan)

Modern Japan

Meiji period or "Restoration": 1868 CE–1912 CE

Taishō period: 1912 CE–1926 CE

Shōwa period: 1926 CE–1989 CE

Heisei period: 1989 CE–2019 CE

Reiwa period: 2019 CE–present

Introduction

Why Japan?

Picture it: Rio de Janeiro, Maracanã Stadium, 2016. As the Rio Summer Olympic Games end, crowds wait to see the Olympic torch handed over to the host country of the 2020 Games, Japan. Familiar icons like Doraemon, Hello Kitty, and Pac-Man join Japanese athletes on stage. Suddenly, Japan's longest-serving prime minister, Abe Shinzo,[1] emerges into the stadium through a green pipe, wearing dungarees and a floppy hat and holding a big red ball in his hands. Almost instantly, his Super Mario costume falls away to reveal Abe dressed in a more conventional sober suit while Tokyo Governor Koike Yuriko, dressed in a kimono, waves a flag with the Olympic rings.

Let's think about this image: The leader of one of the most powerful nations in the world dressed both in a modern, Western-style suit and as a video game character, contrasted with the most powerful woman in Japan dressed in traditional kimono. The red ball Abe holds is a featured centerpiece of the 2020 Tokyo Olympics logo that many have criticized as evoking the rising sun imagery of the Japanese empire. In just this brief moment, we see much of the history of modern Japan: the tension, or, alternatively, "fusion," between popular and traditional culture, the struggle of becoming modern while remaining "Japanese," and a fraught relationship with the past that continues to be publicly debated. As Abe and Koike invite the world to Tokyo in 2020, none of this is lost on the student of Japan.

How do we begin to understand modern Japan, to reconcile the Japan of Pearl Harbor with the Japan of Pikachu? Within just the last century and a half, the country has seen immense and multiple changes in its government, economy, and society. We can pose the same question from another perspective by asking what studying the politics and government of Japan might contribute to understanding democracy in its many forms throughout the world. Japan is, after all, one of the first and most successful cases of non-Western democratic state-building in history, and the first country to develop prosperity and civil liberties comparable to Western European and North American nations. As the world grapples with rising, widespread authoritarianism, perhaps no question is more important.

In a comparative context, some elements of Japan's system of politics may seem familiar, such as a bicameral legislature, regularly held elections, and a prime minister as head of the government. But much is also unique, including an emperor whose family is the world's most long-lived, continuous hereditary monarchy, and a constitution that is, in some ways, more liberal than that of the United States, and in others, more conservative. This volume takes the perspective that understanding political processes can offer a more holistic understanding of modern Japan. Perhaps more than any other East Asian culture, Japan is a highly rule-bound society, and Japanese politics is the art of knowing, bending, and exploiting those rules. At the same time, understanding the development and maintenance of democratic institutions and practices in Japan can offer students of government insight into how democracy works—and doesn't, for that matter— and can illustrate the fact that strengthening democratic institutions is an ongoing struggle *everywhere,* including Japan.

Even though the majority of this book focuses on assisting students and instructors to understand contemporary Japanese politics and government, the beginnings of a political culture were present one thousand years ago, and traces of that political culture can be discerned in politics today. The first chapter includes brief descriptions of early Japan and the advent of shoguns, and then provides a more extensive treatment of governing structures and major governmental reforms beginning with the Tokugawa and—most notably—Meiji periods, ending shortly before the creation of the 1947 constitution.

The second chapter examines the process of creating the postwar constitution, especially General MacArthur's role, the controversies this constitution created immediately upon its enactment, and the continuing calls for revision from across the political spectrum. The third chapter examines how the statutes of the 1947 constitution are put into actual practice. Moving from an introduction to the postwar multiparty system to distinctive aspects of Japan's electoral process (such as *koenkai,* or "support groups," and the blend of single-seat constituency and proportional representation), this chapter introduces readers to the primary political parties in Japanese politics and their platforms.

Often, scholars and political analysts assert that elite bureaucrats actually govern Japan. The fourth chapter explores this claim by focusing on the role bureaucrats play in planning and implementing public policies and the balance of decision-making power between bureaucrats and politicians. The fifth chapter highlights the roles, both informal and professional, played by civil society, and discusses critical issues in domestic politics, including the economy, population decline, and immigration.

The sixth chapter frames key issues in Japanese foreign relations, including the Treaty of Mutual Cooperation and Security with the United States. This discussion will also introduce regional issues such as the rise of China and Japan's response, disagreements over maritime territories, and growing ties in Southeast Asia, along with the increased decision-making power of the Ministry of Defense in these matters. The chapter will also take an international perspective by discussing Japan's role in international peacekeeping missions as part of a broader public or "soft" diplomacy initiative coordinated with the Japan International Cooperation Agency, as well as expanding relations with the Middle East, Europe, and Africa.

The final chapter offers observations on the practice of democratic governance in Japan and its main controversies, returning to key demographic, economic, and social challenges that will likely influence Japanese politics and government in the coming decades. The chapter ends with projected future trends in democracy and governance in Japan and discusses the country's relevance in the region and the world.

Our attempt to understand Japan's government and politics and to compare and contrast Japan with other democratic systems is aided by a working definition of the often misunderstood terms "politics" and "policies." We define "politics" here as the struggle for decision-making power over a group, and "policies" as the intentions or actions that emerge from this process of political struggle. Understanding this process and its outcomes—and the various stakeholders, tools, and institutions that enable and constrain it—is key to understanding modern governance in Japan. At the same time, we should also acknowledge that politics can be reactive, and, in spite of our best efforts, some political elements remain unpredictable. When Abe and Koike took the Olympic center stage in 2016, they could not have anticipated the global COVID-19 health pandemic that would throw governments around the world into crisis and shutter international borders just as Japan was supposed to be opening its own Olympic doors four years later. It would have been similarly difficult to foresee the tragic July 2022 shooting of Abe Shinzo, especially given the fact that Japan has some of the strictest gun control policies and the lowest levels of gun-related violence in the world. In the end, unpredictability and political change may be some of the few constants we do have; if so, a firm grounding in comparative knowledge can help us navigate uncertain futures, even as political sands shift beneath our feet.

1

POLITICAL FOUNDATIONS, THE TOKUGAWA PERIOD, MEIJI REFORMS, DEMOCRATIC ROOTS

Much of Japanese history features periods of borrowing and adapting. All societies borrow from others, whether it's ideas or practices, but Japan is distinct in the extent to which it has selectively borrowed and adapted foreign ways. This process began when Japan borrowed many aspects of Korean and Chinese culture. Chinese influences, transmitted first to Korea and then to Japan from Korea, were present as early as 522 CE with Buddhism's introduction. In subsequent eras such the Nara period (710–794) and especially the Heian period (794–1185), Japanese elites directly learned from China but modified these Chinese ideas and retained uniquely Japanese cultural propensities and institutions. This process of intensely borrowing at times from foreign cultures but building unique Japanese cultural forms repeated itself during the Meiji Restoration (1868–1912), when Japan looked to the US and Western Europe, and again when it looked to the West, especially the US, in the years following the end of World War II. While these periods of reform drastically altered the country's political system and society, Japan is also distinct in that it does not necessarily reject ideas or practices from earlier periods of its own history.

Each new period produces new ideas, institutions, and norms that integrate with earlier practices. When Buddhism came to Japan in the late 6th century, for example, a pantheistic belief system developed that would accommodate Buddhism as well as the indigenous religious beliefs that would eventually become Shintōism along with Confucianism. With this is mind, students will find a historical context of political systems and reform useful to their understanding of modern Japanese politics.

Early Japan, the Emergence of Shoguns, and the Tokugawa Period

Some of the most important elements that came to Japan from China via Korea during the Classical period include Buddhism, Confucian ethical and political thought, a writing system, and a centralized, imperial state. By the time of the Asuka period (538–710), Japan had coalesced into a number of independently ruled kingdoms. Land reforms nationalized and redistributed land equally among farmers, requiring a new national registry be created to reform the tax system with the ultimate goal of centralizing the country into a unified state governed by an emperor. Chinese emperors ruled with a "Mandate of Heaven" and believed their right to rule was given by a divine force. Through this mandate, the emperor played the key role in linking the human social order to the cosmic order. This meant, theoretically, that Chinese emperors could be held responsible if their policies violated the Mandate of Heaven. Japan's political elites modified this system by grounding the emperor's mandate in existing Japanese mythical traditions and a dynastic family lineage. In this mythology, the sun goddess, Amaterasu, sent her grandson, Jimmu, to rule Japan. All descendants of the first emperor, Jimmu, were to be regarded as the imperial family, as deities, and were to rule Japan eternally. In practice though, this resulted in a system where Japanese emperors, unlike their Chinese counterparts, had influence but did not have actual responsibility to rule.[1]

Following Confucian ideas of moral and virtuous leadership and a system that was already in place in Sui dynasty China (581–618), Prince Shōtoku (574–622) introduced a cap and rank system that rewarded officials for individual achievement based on the Confucian values of virtue, benevolence, propriety, sincerity, justice, and knowledge. With a writing system adapted from Chinese characters—ideographic symbols—along with hiragana and katakana phonetic alphabets, bureaucrats developed a system of record keeping and centralized administration.

Many state-administered Buddhist temples were built following an imperial decree promoting Buddhism in 594. Emperors gave Buddhist monasteries free land and an exemption from taxation in their eagerness to have a blessing on their reign, which resulted in many monasteries becoming economically and politically powerful. These religious institutions were also important parts of community life, offering schools, libraries, and resources for the needy. Monks participated in building and infrastructure projects such as roads and irrigation systems, and they received large donations from the public. The extent of the monasteries' influence eventually became an issue of concern for the imperial government, which passed a set of laws in the eighth century to limit the power of Buddhist temples and charismatic priests. Moving the capital from Nara to Kyoto in the Heian period was, in part, to escape the powerful influence of Buddhist priests in Nara.

By the sixth century, Japan was a loosely organized state consisting of territorial entities ruled by clans located in the central region of modern-day Kansai. These

Figure 1.1. Depiction of a bearded Emperor Jimmu with his emblematic longbow and an accompanying wild bird. Source: Tsukioka Yoshitoshi (1839–1892), f rom the series *Mirror of Famous Generals of Great Japan: 1876–1882*. Funatsu Chûjirô (Japanese), Tokyo Metropolitan Library, https://en.wikipedia. org/wiki/Portal:Ancient_Japan#/media/File:Emperor_Jimmu.jpg.

clans competed with each other for power and influence, with the superior family emerging as the imperial family. Though emperors were supposed to have supreme rule of the land, real authority transferred to those who ruled in the name of the emperor, where it stayed for most of Japanese history. By the time of the Heian period, the Fujiwara clan had emerged as the most influential political family by forming ties to the imperial family through marriage, thus allowing Fujiwara family members to act as regent to many generations of emperors and to hold other important political positions. While the government was bureaucratic in theory, it was actually aristocratic since people held positions because of privilege of birth. To some degree, this system produced political continuity and stability even as emperors changed over the years. The Fujiwara clan patronized the arts, and classical Japanese culture, particularly art, poetry, and literature, flourished during the Heian period with the capital located at Kyoto. This period produced the world's first novel, written by Murasaki Shikibu in the eleventh century. *The Tale of Genji*, set at the imperial court, chronicles the experiences of the emperor's son, Genji, as he encounters many different women from varying social backgrounds.

This period of Japanese history is often celebrated as an era of refinement and sophistication, a time when classical Japanese culture was brought to its zenith. But court society was highly elite, representing less than 1 percent of the Japanese population of the time. While Murasaki's *Genji* offers a picture of opulent court life, we do not hear similar stories describing the life of the average person during this time. Most people were illiterate and worked in agriculture or in trades that had developed to serve the court and aristocracy. As the power of the Fujiwara declined and the administrative capacity of the central government weakened, rebellions against the Heian government formed in the provinces. These were led by private landowners, known as *daimyō*, and their armies of warriors, or *samurai*. Clashes between warrior clans for political power culminated in the Genpei War (1180–1185) when the Minamoto clan defeated the Taira clan and established the Kamakura shogunate (1185–1333). Under this government, Minamoto no Yoritomo established himself shogun in 1192 and ruled Japan from the city of Kamakura. Yoritomo remained shogun until his death in 1199, after which his wife and the father of the Hojo clan appointed themselves by creating the position of shogunal regent. In this arrangement, the regent possessed real power, while the shogun operated mainly as a figurehead. Nine successive members of the Hojo family acted as regent until the end of the Kamakura period in 1333.

The conflict that began at the end of the Heian period continued until the beginning of the seventeenth century. This was a time of significant bloodshed and destruction, with natural disasters like earthquakes, tsunamis, and floods as well as fires, famine, and epidemics worsening the effects of the civil war. During the Sengoku or "Warring States" period (1467–1615), Japan splintered into dozens of independent states that were constantly at war with one another. Samurai services were in high demand, as well as the services of ninja, who specialized in unconventional warfare. As those with the most military might swallowed up more and more of their rivals, land became concentrated into fewer and fewer daimyō hands A weak central government and administrative upheaval amid decades of civil war meant Japan was no longer unified but rather a patchwork of feudal states built around fortified castles. Villages and small towns formed their own makeshift local governments in the absence of leadership from a central government.

People increasingly turned to religion for comfort and help in understanding these difficult times, and Buddhism became especially popular. As Buddhism spread, sects such as Pure Land or Lotus Sutra Buddhism emerged that offered followers salvation and release from earthly suffering through faith. These sects, promoted by charismatic monks, appealed to average citizens in a way that the religion of scholars and priests had not. Though governments had long used Buddhism to legitimize various reigns, the reformist nature of some of the new sects drew suspicion, and often hostility, from rival sects and from the government itself. The Nichiren movement in particular promoted its version of the Lotus Sutra, claiming its adoption would save the nation from imminent threats. However, when the world-conquering Mongols attempted to invade Japan twice (in 1274 and 1281), only to be repelled by strong typhoon winds dubbed *kamikaze*—"divine wind"—it was Shinto priests who were richly rewarded for conjuring these protective deities.

Buddhism also spread by *sōhei*, warrior monks associated with the Tendai sect of Buddhism, who protected temples and fought in bitter feuds between rival temples. In Kyoto, sōhei of the Enryakuji Temple were known for burning and destroying temples of rival sects, burning one temple whose founder had split from Enryakuji six times. For five hundred years, neither the imperial court in Kyoto nor the military government in Kamakura could control the Enryakuji armies. Meanwhile, in the provinces, a new kind of sōhei emerged that followed the Jōdo Shinshū sect and called themselves *Ikkō-ikki* ("devoted league"). The Ikkō-ikki, made up of priests, farmers, and families, incited a rebellion against samurai rule and soon established itself in multiple provinces. The success and determination of the Ikkō-ikki attracted the attention of Oda Nobunaga (1534–1582) and Tokugawa Ieyasu (1543–1616), warlords who would defeat both the Enryakuji sōhei and Ikkō-ikki and eventually unite Japan after centuries of civil war.

Figure 1.2. A page from the fifteenth-century century book *O Uma Jirushi* by *Kyūan*, depicting different types of *Uma-jirushi* (heraldic flags used in medieval Japanese warfare). Source: https://commons.wikimedia.org/wiki/File:O_Uma_Jirushi_1.jpg.

Near the end of the sixteenth century, three famous daimyō—Oda and Tokugawa, along with Toyotomi Hideyoshi (1537–1598)—spearheaded unification efforts. After centuries of internal warfare and a decisive victory at the battle of Sekigahara in 1600, Tokugawa Ieyasu established a feudal system that would remain in place until the Meiji Restoration in 1868. As shogun, Tokugawa moved the political capital from Kyoto to Edo (modern-day Tokyo) and relegated the emperor (who stayed in Kyoto) to a largely ceremonial and powerless role. The shogun further awarded daimyō vast holdings of land throughout Japan. In previous feudal eras, daimyō had hired samurai to defend the lands. During the relatively peaceful Tokugawa years, the samurai gradually lost their military function and became bureaucrats or imperial advisers. Shogun, daimyō, and samurai were at the top of the social hierarchy during the Tokugawa years, and peasants, artisans, and merchants constituted the rest of the neo-Confucian official classes, with merchants considered the least esteemed group. In keeping with tradition, merchants were often scorned because they did not make or produce any tangible goods—to the extent that laws were passed to prevent merchants from displaying their wealth. Although this regulation was sometimes enforced rigorously, a number of merchant, artisan, and even some peasant entrepreneurial and manufacturing families became wealthy since, despite the neo-Confucian social order, substantial de facto economic freedom helped to stimulate premodern economic growth.

In the domain system, daimyō were the local authorities possessing fiscal and military autonomy, and they were expected to keep peace in the case of peasant riots. These regional daimyō in turn served a central authoritarian government in Edo known as *bakufu*. This entire feudal political arrangement was known as the *bakuhan*—"*baku*" coming from "bakufu," and "*han*" referring to the roughly 250 domains with two separate bureaucracies required to maintain a system in which two distinct levels of government existed independently. To preserve this political equilibrium between local and central power, the bakufu instituted various control policies. The isolationist *sakoku* policies of the 1630s, for example, formally restricted trading practices with other states save for Dejima, a small artificial island in Nagasaki Bay designated as the forced domicile for Dutch merchants and the site for all trade functions with the Japanese. The sakoku edicts prevented the movement of foreigners, and especially Europeans, in and out of Japan, with the exception of a few Dutch traders who were occasionally allowed with Japanese overseers to visit Edo to present gifts to the shogun. The sakoku policies allowed the shogunate a virtual monopoly over foreign trade and affairs, but especially in Kyushu, in southern Japan, private, often clandestine trade continued with Southeast Asia through most of the period with support from local Kyushu authorities.

A key element to maintaining power was control over the domains. The shogunate employed an extensive spy and police network meant to discourage and report any potentially subversive activity among the daimyō. The domain and castles of daimyō were limited in size and could be reduced as a punishment for suspicious activity. The *sankin-kōtai* system required daimyō to alternate living between their domain and the capital, an expensive migration that drained the resources and time of the daimyō. These restrictive policies together meant that the Tokugawa shogunate enjoyed control over both domestic and foreign matters. It is important to note that although the Tokugawa government would have preferred to instigate even more sweeping totalitarian powers over Japan, there were enough powerful daimyō to dissuade this kind of policy, especially in Kyushu, and Tokugawa military forces were not strong enough to enforce extensive regulations.

The years of Tokugawa rule that brought about the unification of Japan under this domain system and centuries of relative peace is sometimes called the "Pax Tokugawa." These years saw the growth of important institutions, among them a variety of educational opportunities in domains, primarily private "temple schools" that taught basic literacy and numeracy to large numbers of children, and Tokugawa-subsidized academies for students that taught more advanced subjects. This helped Japan enjoy literacy rates that rivaled those of the US and the United Kingdom by the early 1800s. Commerce and manufacturing flourished. Theater, poetry, art, and music created a new urban culture and, for the first time, people who now lived in urban areas had the means and time to pursue leisure and enjoyment. These years of economic, social, and cultural invigoration were the product of national peace, unity, and the creation of strong institutions, including a private commercial and artisan sector, yet these same processes also created the preconditions for the downfall of the Tokugawa regime.

Although the shogunate attempted to avoid outsider incursions, by the middle of the nineteenth century, American and European envoys began arriving on Japanese shores in ships and with technologies that were clearly superior to anything the Japanese possessed. When United States Commodore Matthew Perry arrived in 1853 in the black-hulled steam frigate *Mississippi*, with other warships and three sailing sloops in tow, it was questionable whether the Tokugawa regime could maintain their claim to governing legitimacy as the "expeller of barbarians."[2] The effectiveness of the shogun's military government further deteriorated with the signing of the unequal Treaty of Kanagawa in 1854, which, among other allowances, gave the US the right to establish a consulate in Shimoda and opened ports at Shimoda and Hakodate. Activist samurai, or *shishi*, began lobbying for their local leaders to take stronger anti-foreign stances, even as it became increasingly clear that repelling foreign powers would be impossible given Japan's comparatively weaker military and its inability to resist the "gunboat diplomacy" of the West.

As the careful balance between the central Tokugawa government in Edo and the regional domains began to shift, the Tokugawa shogunate was also significantly challenged by its own inflexibility. The large Satsuma and Chōshū domains of southern Japan would unite to form the Satchō Alliance in 1866 with the aim of removing the Tokugawa regime from power. Peasants had also become more politically active throughout the Tokugawa period, often lobbying for fair taxes

Figure 1.3. Emperor Meiji in Western-style military dress, 1888. Source: https://en.wikipedia.org/wiki/ Emperor_Meiji#/media/File:Meiji_tenno1.jpg.

and benevolent rule.[3] In Osaka, for example, people upset over high taxes, famine, and poor services destroyed a quarter of the city in the 1830s.[4] The indebted and ossified Tokugawa government, often referred to as "wooden monkeys," was falling out of favor just as enthusiasm for imperial leadership was revived under the slogan "*Sonnō jōi*" ("Revere the Emperor, Expel the Barbarians"). Shogun Tokugawa Yoshinobu tried to reform the aging shogunate into a Western-style, multilevel power-sharing system, but these efforts were met with resistance elements of the government that were determined to hold on to power. After a period of struggle, the final Tokugawa shogun, Yoshinobu, abdicated political power to the fourteen-year-old Emperor Meiji in late 1867. The Boshin War (1868–1869) followed, in which Tokugawa loyalists fought against younger samurai and other factions who wanted to return political power to the Imperial Court. Though Emperor Meiji would declare imperial rule restored in 1868, it would not be until late 1869 that the last of the Tokugawa loyalists were defeated and ousted from power.

THE MEIJI RESTORATION AND THE CREATION OF A MODERN JAPANESE STATE

The roots of the modern Japanese political system can be traced to a period of dynamic growth and reform termed the Meiji era (1868–1912). What makes the progress of the Meiji era so pronounced is the stark contrast it provides to preceding centuries, during which Japan was relatively isolated from the outside world, militarily weak, and technologically deficient. Technological advances in the agricultural sector, combined with land reform, created higher yields and greater tax revenues, which the Meiji government invested into manufacturing and industry. After an early and failed experiment with socialism, the Meiji government created a system of state- assisted capitalism that fostered economic incentives for private entrepreneurs to create hundreds of new firms that fueled Japan's economic development. Railroads began to cross the nation, shipping capabilities expanded, and in 1869, the first telegraph line was constructed between Tokyo and Yokohama. The development of a modern banking and finance system further propelled economic growth. The population increased, and many people moved from rural areas to cities. Western fashion, entertainment, and culture increased in popularity. The Japanese army and navy modernized under the national slogan "*Fukoku Kyōhei*," or "rich country, strong army," and won wars against China and Russia. The Meiji era was a time of both nationalism and internationalism as Japan rose quickly to great power status.

The policies of the Meiji era provide an instructive lesson in "modern" state building as Japan now looked to American and European constitutional systems. This was not the first time Japan would adopt a style of government originating beyond its own borders. Chinese systems based on Confucian and Buddhist principles were predominant models for emulation at the height of Chinese imperial power, but the nineteenth century saw power and influence shift westward toward constitutional republics based on ideas from the European

Figure 1.4. A Meiji era *ukiyo-e*, or woodblock print, by Utagawa Kuniteru depicting a steam locomotive at the Yokohama seaside (1874). A port filled with ships flying international flags fills the background, while pedestrians in both Japanese and Western dress mill in the foreground. Source: https://commons. wikimedia.org/wiki/Category:Utagawa_Hiroshige_III#/media/File:Yokohama_Railway_1874.jpg.

Enlightenment. Japan's willingness to learn and adapt is illustrated by the young Meiji emperor's letter to US President Ulysses S. Grant in 1871, delivered on the Iwakura diplomatic mission:

> It is our purpose to select from the various institutions prevailing among enlightened nations such as are best suited to our present conditions and adapt them in gradual reforms and improvements of our policy and customs so as to be upon an equality with them.[5]

Grasping Japan's transformation during the Meiji era begins with an understanding of the term "modern state," a notion that comes to us from seventeenth-century Western Europe. The 1648 Treaty of Westphalia ended the Thirty Years' War in Europe, a conflict that began between Protestant and Catholic states in the Holy Roman Empire but grew to involve most of the great powers of the time. The treaty established a new precedent in Europe of recognizing another state's sovereignty, their right to self-govern without outside interference. The principle of sovereignty would usher in an age of relations between nation-states and would later inform the foundational ideas behind international law.

The concept of statehood is rooted in Westphalian ideas of sovereignty, both internal and external. External sovereignty refers to the ability to occupy and defend a defined territory, while internal sovereignty is the recognition of the state as the sole authority that can make and enforce laws within a defined territory. In the late nineteenth century, modern statehood required an industrialized economy to support a strong military, a centralized government, and a citizenry with a strong national identity. In some ways, the Westphalian system's focus on absolute sovereignty differed from the status quo practices of East Asia, where territorial ambiguity was tolerated and even preferred since not all territories were inhabited or valuable in terms of natural resources. China had long played a predominant role in facilitating trade and diplomatic relations in East Asia, but a weakening nineteenth-century Qing dynasty had become increasingly ineffective at warding off imperial advances from Western powers. To those in power in Meiji Japan, it seemed that gaining equal footing with the predominant world powers would require playing the game by their rules.

In addition to, but distinct from, a modern military and a productive economy is the question of governing legitimacy, which is, simply put, the moral justification for the right to govern. For much of Japanese history since the Kamakura period, emperors lived in relative comfort and safety and were content to play the role of revered spiritual figures. During the Tokugawa period, the emperor in Kyoto was separated from the seat of power in Edo and completely removed from direct exposure to the populace. For hundreds of years, no one except nobility saw the emperor outside the palace.[6] This detachment fueled a mythology surrounding the figure of a divine emperor who could supposedly trace his lineage back to the founding of Japan. This perception was further encouraged by the state adoption of Shinto ideology during the Meiji period as a nation-building tool that affirmed the divinity of the emperor. Though Emperor Meiji's public image as a military figure and political leader made him a symbol for Japan's modernization and an important source of nationalist sentiment, it was always from the imperial family and its supposedly divine lineage that the emperor drew his legitimacy to rule. In practice, however, the emperor did not govern directly, wielded no real political power, and was instead expected to accept the advice of a small number of advisers who played a central role in the overthrow of the shogun.

The first document to outline how the Meiji government would pursue modernization was the Charter Oath, which was presented in April of 1868, a time when there was considerable uncertainty about how the new regime would govern Japan. The Charter Oath maintained there would be the establishment of a deliberative assembly (Article 1) and that all classes of people would unite to "vigorously" carry out the administration of the affairs of state (Article 2). Article 3 would be the basis for further urbanization, as it allowed for everyone to pursue "their own calling." The fourth article promised the "evil customs of the past" would be abandoned in favor of an order based on the "just laws of Nature," though it was deliberately ambiguous whether this was a reference to European social contract theorists like Locke and Rousseau or to Confucian ideas of natural law, which stressed filial piety and loyalty.

The fifth article of the Charter Oath of 1868 both affirmed the position of the emperor and began the practice of sending Japanese citizens to other countries, mainly in the West, to seek out knowledge to "strengthen the foundations of imperial rule." The most well-known of the Meiji-era missions to the West was the Iwakura Mission, a diplomatic voyage to the United States and Europe between 1871 and 1873, which was named after ambassador Iwakura Totomi. Impressed by what they saw, the delegates returned to Japan to promote an industrialization policy that required aggressive state-assisted entrepreneurialism and intense capital investments. The government then created incentives that enabled private owners to achieve impressive economic growth but rejected the Anglo-American model of laissez-faire capitalism—in effect creating a new model of state-assisted capitalism. Meiji leaders invited already successful wealthy families to build upon or start vital industries by establishing private parent companies with subsidiaries that enjoyed oligopolistic positions in the early twentieth century. These *zaibatsu*, or business conglomerates, grew increasingly influential in politics, especially in terms of regional and foreign policy following the First Sino-Japanese War (1894–1895) and the Russo-Japanese War (1904–1905). Reform of the education system also brought skills and literacy to rural areas and to women, which contributed to economic and social development. As heavy industries like shipbuilding took off, the per capita growth rates of Japanese Gross Domestic Product (GDP) outpaced those of almost every major world power during the same period.[7]

One of the most important characteristics of a modern state is the legal monopoly of the use of force. The imperative for industrialization and economic growth was clear in the Meiji-promoted slogan "*Fukoku Kyōhei*," or "rich country, strong army." Japan relied on Western European models as it began to remake and modernize its military. The Conscription Law of 1873 required all men in their twenties to enlist in the Imperial Army. New military education, technologies, and the growing number of conscripts who were compulsorily drafted quickly strengthened the Japanese army and navy. By 1895, Japan had won its first major conflict against China, solidifying Japan's influence in Korea, and it subsequently colonized Taiwan. A costly victory against the Russians during the Russo-Japanese War and participation in World War I on the side of the Allies marked Japan as a major military power. By 1905, Japan had replaced China as the predominant regional power.

The pressure to reform and centralize government stemmed from both domestic and international concerns. The Freedom and People's Rights Movement (eventually the Public Party of Patriots, or *Aikoku Kōtō*), led by Itagaki Taisuke and heavily influenced by French political thought, was gaining support in its demands for a more transparent and democratic government and for the renegotiation of unequal treaties signed with the US and European powers. Simultaneously, the security Japan once enjoyed because of its geographic isolation was eroding as the Western presence continued increasing in East Asia. These dual pressures drove many of the policies that moved Japan from a system of feudalism to a parliamentary style of government at an astonishing pace.

These political reforms began with the dismantling of the Tokugawa feudal system. Hans became "prefectures," daimyō became nonhereditary governors, and samurai—many of whom had already been serving as powerful local bureaucrats since the mid-1800s—lost their class privileges with the institution of a military academy in 1870. While the 1868 Charter Oath invited limited political participation from the domains, Satsuma, Chōshū, Tosa, and Hizen were overrepresented in the *Dajōkan*, Japan's governing body. Controversies bolstered support for pro-democracy movements, which were critical of the new central government's "bureaucratic tyranny" and demanded, among other things, the establishment of a national assembly elected by the people.[8] Thus, the adoption of constitutionalism was in response to domestic pressures for reform, a far from peaceful international environment, and Japan's ongoing pursuit to find equal footing with Western powers.

THE MEIJI CONSTITUTION AND "TAISHO DEMOCRACY"

We have discussed the domestic and international pressures for governmental reform, but we should also consider the 1889 Meiji Constitution from a comparative perspective. The nineteenth century featured a world system centered on Europe and North America. This "centering" included the widespread adoption of Western political norms and institutions meant to create unified nation-states (a concept that was itself a product of Western Europe). The nineteenth century in Europe was also an age of constitutions, many of which were the result of revolutions or clashes between monarchs and feudal leaders. While many European states only

Figure 1.5. Itagaki Taisuke featured on the Japanese 100 yen note printed between 1953 and 1974. Source: https://commons.wiki-media.org/wiki/File:SeriesB100Yen_Bank_of_Japan_note.jpg.

reluctantly adopted new constitutions that limited royal authority, by contrast, the government of Japan was proactive in crafting the Meiji Constitution. Meiji leaders saw constitutional systems not just as contracts for power sharing but also as symbols of a civilized, modern nation.

Itō Hirobumi (1841–1909), Japan's first modern prime minister, was a crucial figure in the creation of the new Meiji Constitution. After returning from a three-year trip to Europe in 1884 to study constitutional systems, Itō chaired the Institutional Research Bureau, a committee tasked with drafting the document that would become the constitution. This constitution was promulgated on February 11, 1889, and it instituted a governing system that had elements of both an absolute and a constitutional monarchy. The emperor was "the head of the Empire" and had "all rights of sovereignty" (Article 4). There was no separation of powers between the sovereign and the legislature, as was common in many Western constitutions; however, the Meiji Constitution also stipulated that, as sovereign, the emperor could choose which of his rights to exercise, "according to the provisions of the present Constitution" (Article 4). The Meiji Constitution publicly granted the emperor enormous power, yet in practice, the exercise of that power was limited and almost always in accordance with the various organs of the state.

The constitution also created the Diet (*Kokkai*), Japan's bicameral legislature, with an upper house, called the House of Peers, and a lower House of Representatives. House of Representative members were elected, though political and voter enfranchisement was severely limited by gender, age, and class. It would not be until 1925 that the lower house was elected by universal suffrage for men over the age of twenty-five. House of Peers members were appointed from among Japan's aristocratic class, of which many members were former daimyō. The power of the Diet, especially the House of Representatives—the body primarily tasked with representing the will of the people—was limited. It could not negotiate over budgetary matters and had no authority over treaties or diplomatic matters. It also required that ministers of state were responsible to the emperor rather than the Diet, and the body had no administrative rights over military matters, which were under the purview of the emperor. The *genrō*, a small group of elder statesmen, reserved the right to appoint the prime minister, who they then advised. While at least two major political parties existed—the liberal-leaning *Kenseikai* and the pro-government alliance of bureaucrats called the *Rikken Saiyūkai*—their inability to unite in the House of Representatives meant they had little leverage in decision-making.

In terms of civil and human rights, the Meiji Constitution had a bill of rights. "Rights" were not conceptualized as inherently human (or natural) rights but instead considered as gifts that flowed from a benevolent emperor. The constitution granted various individual freedoms, including freedom of speech or religion, and civil liberties in general, but they were limited by laws. Likewise, the Meiji Constitution created an independent judiciary, but from the framers' perspective, "the Sovereign is the fountain of justice, and His judicial authority is nothing more than a form of the manifestation of the sovereign power."[9] Voting rights were limited to around 5 percent of the total population. All local authorities were appointed by the emperor, whose choices were advised by the genrō.

In the end, the Meiji Constitution was an attempt at a compromise between Western-style liberal democracy and traditional Japanese autocracy. While the bakuhan system and the strict social hierarchy of the Tokugawa era were abolished, an oligarchic central government retained extensive power over all domestic and international politics. The Meiji Constitution granted only limited civil and political rights to citizens. Most importantly, significant power was vested in the figure of the emperor who was advised by the genrō, a small group with whom real power resided. When Emperor Meiji died in 1912, there was a great deal of uncertainty regarding the future of Japan. Meiji's successor, Emperor Taishō, had contracted cerebral meningitis at an early age, and illness plagued him for most of his life. By 1919, the emperor's illness prevented him from performing any official duties. Power then transferred from the old oligarchic advisers to the Diet and to Taishō's first-born son, Hirohito, who became prince regent. Despite this uncertainty in leadership, modernization efforts continued during the Taishō era (1912–1926), and Japan enjoyed a climate of political liberalism previously unseen in the decades of Meiji. Literary societies flourished with new mass-audience publications, and labor unions organized to protest workforce inequalities. People gathered to protest Japan's involvement in World War I, its treaty negotiations, and its military presence in Manchuria. A class of Japanese women emerged as working-class urbanites, following Western fashions and lifestyles and earning the nickname "modern girls." A movement for women's suffrage and greater democratic representation in general gained support.

This era of liberal optimism, often referred to as "Taishō democracy," came to a halt in September of 1923, when the Great Kanto earthquake devastated the entire

Figure 1.6. Emperor Meiji in a formal session of the House of Peers. Source: Ukiyo-e woodblock print by Chikanobu Yōshū, 1890, https://en.wikipedia.org/wiki/House_of_Peers_(Japan)#/media/File:Y%C5%8Dsh%C5%AB_Chikanobu_House_of_Peers.jpg.

city of Tokyo, including the Port of Yokohama. The earthquake and subsequent fires killed more than 150,000 people and left 600,000 homeless. Martial law was immediately instituted but could not stop the looting and mob violence that followed, much of which targeted Korean ethnic minority populations after rumors circulated they were poisoning water.[10] The Imperial Army used the social unrest as an excuse to arrest and detain political activists they believed were planning to overthrow the government. Power shifted again from the Diet back to the emperor but in name only. In practice, all military decisions were actually made by the prime minister and high-ranking cabinet officials. With little governing power, the Diet would be easily overruled in the 1930s as Japan moved toward a system of ultranationalist totalitarianism.

FROM IMPERIALISM TO POST-WORLD WAR II DEMOCRACY

Developments during the Meiji era, particularly the modernization of the military and a Diet with little power to control it, would contribute to the ultimate downfall of the Japanese empire. By the 1920s, Japan's military had grown exponentially in size and power, defeating China and Russia and participating on the side of the Allied Powers in World War I. One of the legacies of the First World War was an international response favoring pacifism, demilitarization, and a move away from nationalist sentiments. By the time of the Taishō era, the Japanese army had been through several rounds of arms reductions and had signed several treaties limiting Japanese naval power. These policies were at odds with military leaders' belief that embracing an imperialist foreign policy was the key to Japan's acceptance as an equal among world powers. This belief was manifested as action in September of

Figure 1.7. Modern girls wearing "Beach Pajama Style," walking down Ginza in 1928. Source: https://en.wikipedia.org/wiki/Modern_girl#/media/File:Kagayama_mogas.jpg.

1931, the early years of the Shōwa era (1926–1989), when the Kwantung Army of Imperial Japan invaded Manchuria after an explosion destroying a section of Japanese-owned railway was blamed on Chinese nationalists. Despite efforts by various prime and foreign ministers to reign in the military, the Kwantung Army continued advancing into Manchuria, and Japan withdrew from the League of Nations as international criticism of the occupation increased.

Political parties were fully formed and had grown in size and influence to be able to hold majorities in the Diet by the late Meiji era, but the assassination of Prime Minister Inukai Tsuyoshi (1855–1932) and the attempted governmental coup d'état by members of the Japanese navy, army, and an ultranationalist civilian group on May 15, 1932, marked the decline of civilian-led political party power. This incident marked the beginning of a period of weakened democracy and rule of law in Japan. With no strong party leadership and almost all of the genrō elderly or deceased, there were no clear, unifying voices to unite the government and the military. Under the Meiji Constitution, the military was free from civilian oversight or administration, and political factions that developed within military ranks made it even more difficult to control, even for military leaders. After more attempted coups and the assassinations of political figures, the Diet acquiesced to demands for increased military funding as Japan began to maneuver to wartime footing. The ascension of Imperial Army General Tōjō Hideki (1884–1948) to the position of prime minister in 1941 paved the path that would end in eventual military confrontation with the United States and the Allied Powers from 1941 to 1945.

The December 1941 Japanese attack on Pearl Harbor in Hawai'i was the next step in Japan's imperial expansion that had begun almost fifty years earlier. Throughout the entire 1930s, the United States had been slow to consider military involvement in international conflict, instead opting in March 1941 through the Lend-Lease Act to provide aid—first to Great Britain and later to China and the Soviet Union—to purchase war supplies. By 1941, however, it was clear Japan did not intend to abandon its expansionist policies; it had signed the Tripartite Pact with Germany and Italy, a neutrality agreement with the Soviet Union, and an agreement with the Nazi-controlled French government that would enable Japanese forces to move into Indochina. In July 1941, the US, the UK, and the Dutch responded by halting negotiations and instituting a full embargo on all exports to Japan, a crippling move considering that the US was the main supplier of oil, steel, and iron to the Japanese military. Unwilling to retreat from Southeast Asia, convinced the US was against further negotiations, and with finite war-making resources, Japan executed an attack on Pearl Harbor on December 7, 1941, killing more than 2,400 Americans and wounding over 1,100 more. The next day, the US declared war on Japan and joined the side of the Allied forces. Fierce fighting ensued in the Pacific as the US and Japan battled for key island strongholds. Since the latter part of the nineteenth century, Japanese soldiers and civilians were taught that death was preferable to surrender, which made Pacific War island battles even more bloody for both sides. Imperial Japan also attracted worldwide notoriety for the fall 1937 "Rape of Nanjing," when, over a six-week period, victorious Japanese killed approximately three hundred thousand soldiers and civilians (this number is according to Tokyo War Crimes evidence, although Chinese and Japanese sources still argue that the numbers are too low or too high).[11] In July of 1945—following devastating Japanese losses at Midway, Iwo Jima, and Okinawa, and after the Potsdam call for Japan's unconditional surrender—a land invasion of Japan seemed imminent. US President Truman weighed Japan's refusal to surrender with the projected casualties of up to a million American lives in

Figure 1.8. Japanese Foreign Affairs Minister Shigemitsu Mamoru signs the Japanese Instrument of Surrender aboard the *USS Missouri* as General Richard K. Sutherland watches, September 2, 1945. Source: Photograph by Army Signal Corps photographer Lt. Stephen E. Korpanty; restored by Adam Cuerden—Naval Historical Center Photo # SC 213700, public domain, https://commons.wikimedia.org/w/index.php?curid=93758525.

further fighting and instead authorized the use of two atomic weapons in the cities of Hiroshima and Nagasaki on August 6 and 9, respectively. These first and only nuclear attacks inflicted well over 200,000 casualties. The final blow came when the Soviet Union violated the neutrality pact and declared war on Japan, thus signaling the impossibility of a conditional surrender for Japan.

The collapse of the Japanese empire was solidified with its unconditional surrender to the Allied forces on September 2, 1945, and the various other surrender ceremonies that followed throughout Japan's remaining holdings in the Pacific. The Japanese homeland that emerged from half a century of imperial conquest displayed extensive damage, physical and otherwise. It has been estimated that the American firebombing raids prior to surrender "destroyed a significant percentage of most of Japan's cities, wiped out a quarter of all housing in the country, made nine million people homeless, killed at least 187,000 civilians, and injured 214,000 more."[12] This is in addition to the destruction and loss of life in Hiroshima and

Nagasaki as a result of two nuclear weapons. Conditions worsened with the 1946 famine as food distribution systems failed, and most Japanese citizens would not see a significant improvement in their living conditions until 1949 or later.[13] For those who had lived to see the end of Japan's last feudal era, the birth of industrialization, and the rise and fall of a powerful Japanese empire in fewer than eighty years, things would get worse before they got better.

2

POSTWAR POLITICAL REFORMS AND THE REMAKING OF JAPANESE DEMOCRACY

The Allied Occupation (1947–1952) produced significant political changes in Japan, chief among them democratization through the creation of a new constitution. Postwar planning first focused on what to do with the current emperor, Hirohito (1901–1989). Some thought Hirohito should be held accountable for Japan's military expansion across East Asia since, under the Meiji Constitution, he possessed absolute power and sovereignty. Others, including US diplomat and Japan expert Hugh Borton, thought that trying and sentencing the emperor in the Military Tribunal for the Far East would be counterproductive to the goals of the occupation; instead, retaining the emperor would be the best means of gaining the cooperation of the Japanese people during the process of extensive reform that was to follow. General Douglas MacArthur, acting as supreme commander of the Allied Powers (SCAP) in the Pacific, agreed with Borton that the emperor should not be tried and that any changes to the role of the emperor could be carried out in the new constitution.

Before World War II, state sovereignty rested with the emperor, though actual power rested with various groups that claimed to speak for the emperor. In the 1930s, the military was the loudest voice and secured virtually all political power for itself. The Allied forces anticipated that the goal of democratizing Japan would require a revised role for the emperor, and the decision to spare Emperor Hirohito from prosecution for war crimes was controversial. There was powerful international sentiment for prosecuting those responsible for wartime aggression, but the extent of the emperor's actual decision-making power during the war was unclear. Hirohito had supported peace negotiations following the Potsdam Conference. Given the symbolic importance of the throne, General MacArthur convinced US President Truman that allowing Hirohito to retain the throne would promote continuity and citizen cooperation. Emperor Hirohito continued his reign until his death in 1989, when his son, Akihito, assumed the Chrysanthemum Throne.

The role of the emperor in Japanese life is now largely symbolic. He is the head of state but has no political power. Some constitutional duties fall to the emperor, such as opening or dissolving Parliament or making various governmental appointments, but these tasks are subject to cabinet or Diet approval. The emperor is expected to perform largely ceremonial duties, such as attending cultural public events. Despite limited political power, the emperor holds an important diplomatic role. The emperor promotes foreign policy abroad as an unofficial diplomat and hosts foreign leaders and dignitaries at home. Emperor Akihito, who served from 1989 until his abdication in 2019, prioritized mending relations with countries that were victims of Japanese aggression during World War II. His successor and son, Naruhito, has spent much of his time as emperor offering messages of hope during the coronavirus pandemic. As his grandfather, Emperor Hirohito,

Figure 2.1. Emperor Naruhito and Empress Masako in 2019. Source: https://commons.wikimedia.org/wiki/File:Emperor_Naruhito_and_Empress_Masako.jpg.

did in 1964, Emperor Naruhito offered a brief speech to open the 2021 Olympic Games hosted in Tokyo. By using the word "commemorate" instead of the more commonly used term "celebrate" in his opening speech, Naruhito paid tribute to the lives lost throughout the COVID-19 pandemic and marked the solemnity of an opening ceremony where live spectators were not allowed.

DRAFTING A NEW CONSTITUTION

Three principles would guide the drafting process of the new constitution. First, sovereignty should rest with the people and not with the emperor, who would function solely as head of state. To this end, in January 1946, Emperor Hirohito issued what is referred to as the "Humanity Declaration" and officially denied any claim to divinity. Second, the right to war would be abolished as an instrument for settling disputes. Third, building on the existing Diet structure, and with British parliament as a model, the system of peerage would be abolished and with it the inherited power of Japan's aristocracy.[1]

There was some disagreement among the General Headquarters of SCAP (GHQ) and Japanese officials over the provisions and drafting of the new constitution. On February 8, 1946, Matsumoto Jōji, chairman of the Constitutional Problems Investigative Committee, presented GHQ with a drafted constitution that barely amended the Meiji Constitution and did not satisfy the Allies' terms in the Potsdam Declaration that governed Japan's surrender. Unbeknownst to the Japanese, the Government Section of GHQ, headed by General Courtney Whitney and which included Colonel Charles Kades, had also been tasked with drafting a new constitution.[2] On February 13, Whitney presented the GHQ version of the constitutional draft. Various drafts were then exchanged between GHQ and the cabinet of Prime Minister Shidehara Kijuro until GHQ pressed the cabinet to accept the "fifth draft," which was very close to the original GHQ version.[3] The cabinet agreed, and the draft constitution was finalized in April of 1946.

Any new constitution would need to be reviewed and approved by the Diet, which would first need to be elected. There had been no true competitive elections in Japan since the military began to consolidate power in the 1930s. The first postwar election in 1946 presented an opportunity for many politicians to return to governing roles and for new groups of people, particularly women, to engage in political participation. Yoshida Shigeru, a former diplomat, joined the conservative-leaning Liberal Party and was appointed prime minister when the Liberal Party won a plurality at the ballot box in April of 1946, but only after the first leader of the Liberal Party, Hatoyama Ichirō, was purged by SCAP under suspicion of support for ultranationalist leaders in the 1930s and 1940s. Yoshida, given his pro-Western proclivities that he gained from his time spent abroad as a diplomat, was an ideal candidate for prime minister in the eyes of the occupying authorities. The Liberal Party then formed a coalition government with the next highest vote-receiving party, the conservative Progressive Party. The Socialist Party, Cooperative Party, and Communist Party, plus a handful of smaller parties, received the remaining votes and formed the opposition. Many of the political parties of postwar Japan were founded the late 1800s but were fluid, as factions merged with and splintered from other parties and built on the remnants of these earlier organizations. The postwar decade of leadership under the Liberal and Progressive Parties would last until the unification of the Japan Socialist Party and the emergence of the Liberal Democratic Party in 1955.[4]

In June of 1946, the Yoshida cabinet presented the draft of the new constitution to the Diet for approval. Immediately, disagreements among members erupted over Article 9 and its provisions for pacifism. GHQ requested the inclusion of language from the Kellogg-Briand Pact, a treaty resolving to renounce war as a means for settling international disputes; Japan was an original signatory in 1928. Some members of the Diet supported the inclusion of this wording in Article 9 as a means of demonstrating Japan's commitment to peace that might hopefully pave the way for Japan's return to its position of trusted global leadership. Others thought the article went too far, leaving Japan vulnerable and without hard power resources for protection. While the charter of the newly formed United Nations aimed to save future generations from the "scourge of war," it also permitted states to maintain military forces for defensive purposes.[5] Though minutes of the special Diet subcommittee meetings on Article 9 do not exist, many (including Charles Kades) claim it was Ashida Hitoshi of the LDP who suggested inserting the phrase, "In order to accomplish the aim of the preceding paragraph." Ashida later asserted the phrase prohibited Japan only from using force as a means to "settle international disputes" while allowing it to use force in self-defense and when participating in UN-approved military operations.[6] The provisions of Article 9 have proven to be a source of continued controversy and interpretation since they were written.

> **Article 9**
>
> (1) Aspiring sincerely to an international peace based on order, the Japanese people forever renounce war as a sovereign right of the nation and the threat or use of force as means of settling international disputes. In order to accomplish the aim of the preceding paragraph, land, sea and air forces, as well as other war potential, will never be maintained. The right of belligerency of the state will not be recognized.
>
> (2) In order to accomplish the aim of the preceding paragraph, land, sea, and air forces, as well as other war potential, will never be sustained. The right of belligerency of the state will not be recognized.
>
> — Article 9, The Constitution of Japan (1947)

Nevertheless, the recently elected Diet approved the constitution in October of 1946, and Emperor Hirohito presented it to the people of Japan in November. The document established the democratic freedoms of assembly, religion, and speech and recognized universal suffrage. Though there had been a vibrant suffrage movement in Japan since the Meiji era and women had participated in elections during the Taisho years, it wasn't until the postwar period that rights for women were constitutionally guaranteed. Women could vote, campaign for, and

Figure 2.2. Some of the thirty-nine women elected to the Japanese Diet in 1946. Source: https://en.wikipedia.org/wiki/Women%27s_suffrage_in_Japan#/media/ File:First_Japanese_Congresswomen.jpg.

hold elected office, and they could enjoy equal rights in matters of marriage and family law such as inheritance and property ownership. The new constitution also tackled land reform and the break-up of the zaibatsu. It stripped the emperor of any political power and made him accountable to and a symbol of the people. The new constitution also forever renounced war as a sovereign right of the nation and provided that no standing military or "war potential" would ever be maintained. It further banned members of the military from serving as prime minister or in a ministerial position, and it placed the military firmly under the authority of democratically elected officials.

US-JAPAN SECURITY TREATY

A revised constitution was not the only document that would shape postwar politics in Japan. Though the Allied Occupation was set to end in 1952 with the San Francisco Peace Treaty, the US was not keen to abandon its strategic military position in East Asia just yet. With the Soviets and the now Communist People's Republic of China nearby and the Korean War still ongoing, Japan was becoming a potential key ally in the US's Cold War containment-focused foreign policy. The US proposed a US-Japan Security Treaty that framed Japan's disarmament as insecurity, a problem that could be remedied by the US pledge to defend Japan in exchange for the right to maintain a large military presence in the country. This arrangement aligned with the prevailing "Yoshida Doctrine" of the time, Prime Minister Yoshida's strategy to let the US take care of security while Japan focused on economic rebuilding.[7] The security treaty was introduced as a part of the San Francisco negotiations, with the US pushing the Japanese delegation to sign the treaty the same day as the official peace treaty. Despite some reluctance to continue

Figure 2.3. 1960 protests against the United States-Japan Security Treaty. Source: From "Album: The 25 Years of the Postwar Era," published by the Asahi Shimbun Company, https://commons.wikimedia.org/wiki/File:1960_Protests_against_the_United_States-Japan_Security_Treaty_02.jpg.

engagement with the US, many leaders at the time felt they had little choice but to acquiesce, and the treaty was signed on September 8, 1951. In 1954, despite strong domestic objections, the Japanese Self-Defense Forces (SDF) emerged from the National Police Reserve and the passage of the 1954 Self-Defense Forces Law. Those objections intensified in May and June of 1960 when the US-Japan Security Treaty was renegotiated as the Treaty of Mutual Cooperation and Security (*Sōgo Kyōryoku Oyobi Anzen Hoshō Jōyaku*, or *Anpo* in shorthand), which gave the US its first permanent foothold in East Asia. Tens of thousands of protestors flooded the streets in Tokyo, ten million people signed petitions protesting the treaty, and US President Dwight D. Eisenhower had to cancel a planned visit to Japan as thousands were injured and one person was killed in the "days of rage and grief."[8] Despite this outcry, treaty ratification was forced through the lower house of the Diet in a special midnight session after police removed opposition legislators who were blocking the session's opening. This spectacle and the general outrage forced the resignation of Kishi Nobusuke, the prime minister at the time.

Constitution and Treaty Controversies

Both the postwar constitution and the security treaty with the US have continued to be sources of varying levels of controversy in Japan. Since its formation in 1955 following a merger of the Democratic and Liberal Parties, the Liberal Democratic Party (LDP) has advocated for constitutional revision, first creating the Commission on the Constitution in 1956. Common criticisms of the constitution were that it was not Japan's constitution but rather "MacArthur's constitution" that was forced on Japan. Other objections have to do with Article 9 and the arguable necessity it created for the continued relationship with the United States. LDP opposition parties—primarily the Socialist and Communist Parties—were hesitant to revise a constitution that had only stood for a decade since its last revision. Despite factional disagreements within the LDP on the wisdom of pushing constitutional changes, the party united against the Socialists and Communists in its support of the security treaty with the US. After the protests and the resignation of Kishi in 1960, the LDP refocused its efforts on less controversial topics, such as economic growth.

It wasn't until political realignment in the 1990s that other parties in addition to the LDP began putting forth suggestions for constitutional revision. In 2000, both the upper and lower houses formed research commissions on the constitution,

Figure 2.4. *Nobori* flags (banners) held by a group of pro-Article 9 demonstrators and their police escort near the Ginza neighborhood of Tokyo. Source: https://en.wikipedia.org/wiki/Article_9_of_the_Japanese_Constitution#/media/ File:Proarticle9demo-may2014nearginza.jpg.

the results of which tried to provide a basis for future discussion but offered no concrete suggestions. Further legislation has since created procedures for holding national referendums, which are a required part of the process to formalize any proposed constitutional amendment that receives a two-thirds majority approval in both houses. Prime Minister Abe Shinzo (1954–2022) made constitutional revision, especially of Article 9, a focal point of his second administration, and he succeeded in reinterpreting Article 9 so as to allow new security legislation. Yet the issue of constitutional revision has yet to move past study and discussion to proposing—let alone passing—amendments.

This hesitancy is unusual compared to the relative frequency with which other democratic nations alter their constitutions. The Republic of Korea's constitution, for example, was adopted in 1948 (just one year after Japan's) and has been amended nine times, most recently in 1987. The topic of constitutional revision has increasingly become intertwined in conversations about general governance reform. While the LDP has historically led the argument for constitutional revision, political realignment has created opportunities for other parties to voice their proposals for constitutional revision as well. By 2005, for example, both the Democratic Party of Japan and the Komeito Party were campaigning with constitutional revision as a part of their platforms.[9] Now that many alternative ideas and proposals exist, the path to revision may be less clear. To build on that reality, the second possible explanation is based on a consideration of the Japanese decision-making technique *nemawashi*, which requires building support for a project or decision in advance to gain consensus. Though more commonly used in business settings to promote communication and harmony, it may also explain the slow and deliberative process of constitutional revision. Japan is a consensus-based society, and nemawashi—"the long and arduous process of building consensus through countless consultations, negotiations, and compromises—sets the foundation for change."[10] Regardless of whether the parties can negotiate, draft, and approve an amendment proposal, the proposal would still need to succeed in a national referendum. Polling from the liberal *Asahi Shimbun* and the conservative *Yomiuri Shimbun* (Osaka and Tokyo-based newspapers, respectively) seems to suggest that a majority of Japanese citizens would not support constitutional revision, though the margins are slim. Russia's 2022 invasion of Ukraine led to increased calls from lawmakers for constitutional revision in order to better deter an attack, but only time will tell whether words of support will become policy.

3

BRANCHES OF GOVERNMENT, POLITICAL PARTIES, ELECTIONS

The 1947 constitution built on the existing governmental bicameral parliamentary structure created by the Meiji Constitution but departed from the Meiji model in key ways. Most significantly, sovereignty would now rest with the people of Japan, and power would be constitutionally guaranteed to a democratically elected legislative body. While the 1947 constitution guaranteed civil and personal freedoms unrivaled outside the most liberal Western regimes, Japanese politics largely remains elitist and, in many ways, inaccessible to citizens.

This chapter examines key institutions of Japanese government, beginning with the three branches of government: judicial, executive, and legislative. The chapter continues with a discussion of elections, political parties, electoral regulations, and electoral reform before concluding with a brief critique of the party system.

JUDICIAL BRANCH

An independent judicial system that enjoys the confidence of the citizenry is central to preserving the rule of law in any country. The term "rule of law" refers to a principle under which all people, institutions, and entities are accountable to laws that are formally declared and which most people are aware of and find to be fair and equitably adjudicated. Judicial systems can interpret and enforce laws, seek justice for those harmed, decide punishments for crimes committed, and act as a check on executive and legislative power. Japan's court system is arranged hierarchically under the umbrella of the Ministry of Justice. Four courts exist below the Supreme Court of Japan: high courts, district courts, family courts, and summary courts. These courts hear civil and criminal cases, family affairs determinations, and judicial appeals. Trials utilize an inquisitorial system, where judges take an active part in seeking out facts by asking questions of the prosecution and the defense. After hearing evidence, judges are the arbiters of ruling and sentencing rather than juries, as is common in the US. In contrast to the US system, which favors justice in process, the Japanese system prefers justice in outcome—that is, finding out who did it and why. Japan's famous "99.3 percent" conviction rate has caused many to wonder whether it is possible for a defendant to get a fair trial. Carlos Ghosn, the former chief executive of Nissan accused of the misuse of corporate assets, fled Japan for Lebanon in 2019, citing concerns he stood no chance of acquittal in a Japanese court.

The number of cases that Japanese courts hear provides a context for the high conviction rate. Thorough and lengthy investigations generally precede prosecutor decisions on whether to take on a case, and cases rarely proceed to trial without a confession. The 2016 Ministry of Justice Annual Report of Statistics on Prosecution found that only 37 percent of the arrest cases made it to trial. For this reason, critics say, prosecutors always have the upper hand because the assumption is they only take cases when the accused is guilty. Proponents of this system cite its efficiency in administering justice since it dismisses cases where there is insufficient evidence, thereby lowering the cost of the legal system and protecting the innocent from unnecessary trial. Critics have called this a "hostage justice" system since Japan's criminal code of procedure allows the accused to be held for twenty-three days without bail, a period of time that can be lengthened with additional charges and during which suspects may be coerced to confess to crimes they did not commit. Investigators are allowed to question suspects without an attorney present, and most interrogations are not filmed or recorded.

Judges are expected to be impartial. But they can potentially take the shortcut of deferring to the prosecution, and they often refuse bail, even when cases do not involve violence or the suspect is not a flight risk. Other criticisms of the Japanese justice system include the continued lack of legal protections against racial, ethnic, or religious discrimination and the country's continued use of the death penalty. Together with the US, Japan is the only Organization for Economic Cooperation and Development (OECD) country that continues to execute prisoners. In an effort to make the judicial system a more welcoming venue for citizens to bring grievances, in 2004, the *saiban-in*, or lay judge system, was introduced.[1] In this system, a judge is chosen from the electorate to assist a professional judge in the process of a case, a policy meant to introduce average citizens to the normally mysterious and rarefied air of the courts, but opinion polls have found that 70 percent of Japanese would be reluctant to serve as a judge.[2]

The Supreme Court, the highest and final court in Japan, is responsible for hearing final appeals of decisions made in the lower courts. The cabinet appoints fourteen Supreme Court justices, and the emperor ceremonially appoints one chief justice after nomination from the cabinet. Supreme Court justices in Japan are subject to review by the public every ten years, though many are appointed in their sixties and retire by seventy, and the court so rarely takes on controversial cases that no judge has ever been removed from their bench. Unlike many other supreme courts, the Supreme Court of Japan does not take an active role in reviewing the constitutional validity of legislation approved by the Diet, a process called judicial review. Before World War II, courts were not independent of the executive; though the Supreme Court now has the constitutional authority of judicial review, it does not often use it. In the six decades following the postwar period, the Supreme Court of Japan struck down eight laws on constitutional grounds, earning it the label of the "most conservative and cautious court in the world" in terms of exercising judicial review; in comparison, during the same period, the United States Supreme Court struck down roughly nine hundred laws.[3] When decisions are rendered that contradict existing policy decided by political branches, it is generally interpreted as the replacement of judges not keeping pace with changes in the sociopolitical climate. Though the constitution gives the Supreme Court the authority to provide checks and balances on the executive and legislative branches, the court rarely does so. Thus, the judicial system does not act as an effective check on the Diet's power.

EXECUTIVE AND LEGISLATIVE BRANCHES: THE PRIME MINISTER AND THE DIET

Japan is a typical unitary parliamentary system in that the party or party coalition who holds a majority in the Diet chooses the chief executive (in this case, the prime minister) from among elected legislators in the House of Representatives, a key distinction from a federal system where the president is independently elected and cannot be a member of the legislature. In the Diet, the prime minister's powers are distinctly separate from that of legislators, and prime ministers have no formal powers without substantial Diet support. There is no formal term of office for Japan's chief executive; rather, it is the House of Representatives that decides when elections will be held for a new prime minister. In the 1990s, this frequently occurred, with several prime ministers leaving office within one to two years. Koizumi Junichiro's five-year term in the early 2000s brought stability, and more recently, Abe Shinzo attained the longest tenure of any prime minister—a brief 2006–2007 tenure, then another one for almost eight years from 2012 to 2020. After Abe's 2020 resignation, Suga Yoshihide served as prime minister for thirteen months until the 2021 general election elevated Kishida Fumio from minister for foreign affairs to prime minister.

The prime minister is head of the cabinet and appoints, as in the US, civilian ministers to head government departments, usually from among lower house members from within his party. The constitution defines clear roles for the cabinet, such as managing foreign affairs, preparing and submitting a budget to the Diet, and administering the civil service of over three million employees, including the Japanese Self-Defense Forces. Cabinet members can lose their positions if a prime minister resigns or if a prime minister "shuffles" their cabinet to shift policy priorities.

The prime minister's greatest constitutional power is the ability to dissolve the lower house and call for a general election—a strategic move, often used to bolster support for controversial issues and strengthen a prime minister's Diet majority. If the lower house is dissolved, either by the emperor on the recommendation of the cabinet, or following a no-confidence vote in the lower house against the cabinet, a general election is mandated within forty days. Lawmakers return to their home districts and again stand in a "snap" election. This may seem chaotic and irregular, but it is a normal part of the political process in most parliamentary systems. In fact, the Diet's lower house representatives have only finished one complete four-year term in the past seven decades.

Lower house dissolution has potential costs and benefits. If the political landscape is favorable, then a majority win in a snap election can push party-favored legislation. In 2005, Liberal Democratic Party (LDP) Prime Minister Koizumi Junichiro called a snap election after losing a vote on a postal privatization bill. The privatization bill passed after the LDP won a landslide majority in the following election. But dissolution can also backfire, as it did in 2012 when Prime Minister Noda Yoshihiko of the Democratic Party of Japan (DPJ) disbanded the lower house after unsuccessful attempts to pass a social security and tax reform bill. His timing could not have been worse, as the DPJ's approval ratings had plummeted following the Fukushima Daiichi nuclear disaster in 2011. Noda's DPJ lost the majority, thus ending his administration and bringing the LDP back to power.

The Japanese Diet, established in 1890, is one of the world's oldest parliaments and the supreme organ of state power. The Diet is bicameral, with an Upper House of Councillors and a Lower House of Representatives.

The Lower House, or the House of Representatives, has 465 seats elected from 129 districts across Japan. Lower House members are elected for four-year terms. If the Lower House passes a bill the Upper House vetoes, the Lower House can override the veto with a two-thirds majority vote. This is why the Lower House is usually considered to be the more powerful of the two houses, though that is true only if there is a consistent voting majority in the Lower House and, in some cases, a supermajority. Most aspiring career politicians tend to prefer election to the Lower House rather than the Upper House since prime ministers and most Cabinet positions will be drawn from the Lower House.

The House of Councillors is a modern version of the Meiji-era House of Peers. Councillors are elected to fixed, six-year terms in staggered elections. The House of Councillors' greatest power is its ability to delay votes on legislative items by returning them to the House of Representatives for a revote. If an item is not approved by the time the Diet session ends, the item "expires" and must start over from square one in the next Diet session. In practice, this does not happen often since the LDP and its longtime coalition partner, the Komeito Party, typically hold a majority in both houses. Though rare, there are instances when the majority

Figure 3.1. National Diet Building of Japan, located in Tokyo. Source:
https://commons.wikimedia.org/wiki/File:Diet_of_Japan_Kokkai_2009.jpg.

party in government and the majority party in the Upper House are different, resulting in a "twisted Diet." This was the case in a 2007 election when the LDP lost Upper House seats to the DPJ, resulting in the resignation of Abe Shinzo, who was then prime minister. The one instance where the Lower House cannot override the Upper House is in a vote to amend the constitution, which requires a two-thirds majority in both houses before moving to the public for a referendum.

POLITICAL PARTIES

The organization and development of political parties as institutions is at the heart of any study of democracy. Modern political parties emerged as a way to organize societies with deep social cleavages. As a result, parties represented groups of people who shared similar values and ideas and wanted to achieve similar goals through political means. Before the easy accessibility of mass media, political parties performed as organizational, fundraising, and informational tools. Today, the government provides public funding for parties to advertise their candidate, and the wide reach of the media, both print and digital, provides information to voters. Perhaps most importantly, social cleavages no longer create party lines; instead, political parties use charismatic politicians to present themselves as appealingly as possible to wide and diverse swaths of the population. As a result, the parties' policy platforms have become increasingly amorphous. Of course, the policy goals of any party are a result of compromise, both among its own diverse membership and in anticipation of working with other parties in government. In Japan, this means it is sometimes difficult to tell how the parties and their candidates differ on issues of actual policy.

The Liberal Democratic Party

The Liberal Democratic Party (LDP) has been at the core of Japanese politics since its formation in 1955 from the merger of two smaller conservative parties. Since 1955, it has held a majority in government—except for ten months in 2003–2004, and from 2009–2012—either on its own or as the dominant party in a coalition. The LDP is a moderate to conservative party, but its ideology often departs from Western counterparts in important ways. Most conservative parties support a limited role for government and strong private and local initiatives, but the LDP often prefers an active, strong, centralized government. The LDP actively worked to rebuild the image of Japan following World War II, doing so almost exclusively through economic rather than military means. These proclivities for economic intervention and administrative guidance are the distinguishing features of Japan's "state-assisted" system. The LDP maintains close ties to business and industry, a relationship that has often resulted in party corruption in addition to economic growth.

The distinguishing institutions of the LDP are the *koenkai* (local support groups) the Policy Affairs Research Council (PARC), factions within the party, and political figures who lead those factions. Party leadership is often exercised through positions in the PARC. In Japan, the cabinet introduces most of the legislation on which the Diet votes. While it is common in parliamentary systems for most legislation to be born through cabinet bills, Japan is unique in that politicians do not play a large role in the drafting process; instead, drafted legislation originates within the bureaucracy and makes its way to the Diet through the cabinet. The Cabinet Legislation Bureau, a government-appointed agency, examines bills, orders, and treaties, and it advises cabinet members on the legality of proposed legislation. An informal agreement struck in the late 1960s attempted to increase party power in drafting legislation. Under this agreement, it is customary, though not legally required, for the LDP Executive Council and the PARC to approve all government-sponsored bills (at least when the LDP is in power, which is most of the time). This gives the chairs of the Executive Council, PARC, and the secretary-general of the LDP enormous power over legislation and over the prime minister, with whom they do not always agree.

Factions, or groups with varying interests from their fellow party members, have existed within the LDP since its formation in 1955. In any party, it is natural for some members to have more in common with one group rather than another—we may point to Alexandria Ocasio- Cortez's "squad" in the US House of Representatives as a progressive faction in the Democratic Party, or the Republican Freedom Caucus led by Representative Scott Perry as a faction of the Republican Party. In contrast, factions in the LDP are institutionalized features of the political organization. Leadership comes from a senior political figure. Factions maintain enrollment lists, though membership is fluid and, therefore, an important source of competition among the political elite. Senior faction members help young politicians make beneficial connections by introducing them to bureaucrats and business leaders. Some factions have formed and dissolved over time, but the original five factions carried over from before the merger of the Liberal and Democratic parties still exist today, and the vast majority of LDP members belong to one of them. Most politicians rise to the position of prime minister by way of factional leadership, and most cabinet appointments align with the relative power of the factions.

One of the most important tools of politicians seeking office, especially in the LDP, has been the koenkai, or local support groups that contribute funds and other support to candidates. In the early 1990s, one in seven voters had an affiliation with a candidate's koenkai.[4] In addition to contributing funds, members may volunteer to send out mailers, make phone calls on the candidate's behalf, or invite the candidate to speak at community events throughout the year, thus providing candidates a way to evade strict campaign regulations. To some extent, koenkai have declined in power due to electoral reform, problems with recruiting younger members, and an increased reliance on the "brand" of the LDP in an age of weakened party identification and loyalty.

Komeito

The Komeito Party has been an important political ally of the LDP for over three decades. A center to center-right party, Komeito was formed as the Clean Government Party from the Soka Gakkai Buddhist movement. Komeito generally supports the policy platform of the LDP, earning criticism that it is little more than a rubber stamp for the LDP. Komeito and the LDP are sometimes misaligned on a few key issues. For one, Komeito was a completely pacifist party when it first formed, though it has since softened its stances and voted in favor of authorizing Japanese action in Iraq and Afghanistan and in favor of Abe's 2014 security legislation. Komeito also tends be more in favor of social spending, like reducing school fees and offering child care allowances, than the LDP. However, despite its smaller numbers, Komeito has exercised power that exceeds its size when there is no consensus among LDP factions. The LDP alone does not have the votes to pass legislation through the Diet, so LDP leaders are often willing to forego suggestions from their own party in favor of those from Komeito. For example, security issues often divide the LDP. When former Prime Minister Abe lobbied for constitutional revision of Article 9, the language in the proposal included a section criticized by members of his own party at Komeito's insistence. Komeito Party leaders have often referred to their party as the "brakes" on the LDP's more aggressive ambitions.

Constitutional Democratic Party, Social Democratic Party, and Democratic Party for the People

An efficient, democratic process requires opposition parties to hold majority parties accountable by acting as a watchdog and by challenging majority opinions. The Democratic Party of Japan provided the most significant opposition challenge to the LDP before gaining control of government from 2009 to 2012. The Constitutional Democratic Party (CDP) is a center-left political party that was formed in 2017 after a split in the Democratic Party of Japan. Many of the long-serving DPJ members joined the CDP, including the left-leaning former prime minister Kan Naoto and the more conservative former prime minister Noda Yushihiko. The CDP is now the strongest opposition party in the Diet to the LDP/Komeito coalition and supports increased government investment in renewables and a phasing out of nuclear energy. The CDP opposes any revisions to Article 9 and any increases in the consumption tax. The Social Democratic Party has been active since 1996, but after losing most of its members to the DPJ, it agreed to a merger with the CDP in November of 2020. Similarly, the Democratic Party for the People is a center to center-right party formed in 2018 that also agreed to merge with the CDP in 2020; however, fourteen DPP members refused to merge and formed a new party retaining the DPP name.

Japan Innovation Party

Formed from a 2015 split in the old Japan Innovation Party, Nippon Ishin no Kai (often just called "Nippon Ishin") has grown from a regional, Osaka-based party to a national party with the second-most opposition seats in the Diet after the CDP. While Nippon Ishin has been called conservative and populist, the party manifesto released for the 2021 general election outlines policies that fall on various points of the political spectrum. Their support for economic liberalization policies, like labor force and industry deregulation, exists alongside support for a universal basic income and free education. Socially, the party supports the legalization of same-sex marriage and separate surnames for married couples. Nippon Ishin largely aligns with the LDP on defense matters, supporting constitutional revision and removing limits on defense spending, but it has also openly discussed Japan joining a nuclear weapons-sharing agreement, a topic long seen as taboo. Many of their other core policies are tied to their origins as a regional party and support political decentralization and increased regional governing power. The Kansai region, and Osaka in particular, remain Nippon Ishin's stronghold of support, and it is yet to be seen whether the party can mobilize its organizational power to increase its national appeal.

Japan Communist Party

The Japan Communist Party (JCP) has the longest history of any political party in Japan. Established in 1922, it is a rare example of a continuing Communist presence in a democratic country. For many years, the JCP has unsuccessfully lobbied for a coalition with the main opposition party to form a united front against the LDP- Komeito alliance. The CDP and JCP agree on many issues: they both oppose nuclear energy and revisions to Article 9. The parties diverge on other important policy matters, however, like the JCP's support for terminating the US-Japan alliance and avoiding membership in regional trade agreements in favor of economic sovereignty.

Elections and Electoral Reform

From 1925 to 1994, a system of single nontransferable voting (SNTV) in multimember districts (MMD) elected Diet members. In this system, a candidate who won the most votes won an open seat. In each district, more than one seat would be available, so the candidate with the second-most votes would win a second seat and so on. Under this system, a party could only win a majority in the Diet by running multiple candidates and winning multiple seats in any given district. To illustrate, if more than five candidates were running in a five-seat constituency, Party A would run as many candidates as possible; while voters only got one vote each, there would still be five candidates elected, and Party A would want as many seats as possible. The weakness of Party A's strategy is that it would force party members to compete with one another, and any Party A candidate that received too many votes would harm the chances of other candidates from Party A, even if that party was the most popular one. This intraparty competition led to factionalism within parties and excessively expensive elections. By the early 1990s, there were calls to reform the electoral system.

The 1994 electoral reforms attempted to eliminate intraparty competition and refocus elections on issues rather than on party positions and the personalities of individual candidates. A semi proportional, parallel system of elections used in other countries like South Korea, Russia, and Taiwan replaced the SNTV system. In this system, voters participate in two separate elections for a single chamber, and the results in one election have little or no impact on the results of the other. In a lower house single-member district (SMD) election, a candidate wins office by gaining a plurality of votes. On the second ballot, voters choose a party in the regional "block" constituency, where election results determine proportional seat allocation. For example, the multimember block constituency for Tokyo elects seventeen members to the lower house proportionally; in 2017, the LDP filled six seats of the seventeen available after receiving roughly 30 percent of the votes. Candidates fill these seats according to their position on a list compiled internally by the parties. In the lower house, party lists fill 176 seats, and 289 are SMD constituency seats. Upper house elections follow a similar parallel procedure of SMD and proportional representation (PR) voting, where the latter accounts for 40 percent of seats, the difference being that a nationwide constituency elects the ninety-six proportional seats, with votes from all over the country tallied together.

Lower House elections allow for dual candidacy, so a candidate can place on a party list and still potentially win a seat even if he or she does not win their race in the SMD election. The most significant criticism of parallel voting is inaccurate representation—big parties can win big majorities. There is a no compensatory mechanism to adjust the *overall* number of seats won by each party to reflect the actual proportion of votes received, and big parties are favored in SMD elections that fill 63 percent of Lower House seats. One attempt to add more voter influence to the party list process is to rank SMD election losers by how well each polled compared to the winner in their district, thus lowering the chances that an unpopular candidate will still gain a seat on general party popularity.

Local Elections

Every four years, voters go to the polls to elect governors and members of assemblies in forty-one prefectures as well as mayors and assembly members in some of the major cities. The Local Autonomy Law divides local and regional governments into two categories: local public entities (LPEs) of forty-seven prefectures in charge of regional administration, and basic municipalities of cities, towns, and villages. These administrative units can range from small villages, like Ōkawa in Kōchi Prefecture, with an estimated four hundred residents, to the large and populous Tokyo Metropolitan Government. One of the unique features of Tokyo, which has over nine million people, is that it includes twenty-three LPEs, referred to as "special wards," and thus has characteristics of both a city and a prefecture. Because Japan is a unitary system with a centralized structure of government, local governments are highly dependent on the national government to meet their budgetary needs. This also means that, while technically autonomous, the national government does have some influence over policy matters at the local level. Again, Tokyo is the exception since it raises enough funds to finance itself and enjoys some policy autonomy.

As is the case in many countries, political issues tend to vary regionally and focus locally. Antinuclear power sentiments are more likely in cities with nuclear reactors, and there are more concerns about immigration in rural, agricultural areas. Local issues and elections can have big effects on national politics too. In Okinawa, the stationing of US troops and the social effects of the military bases located there are often central issues in local and prefectural elections. In 2009, the DPJ won in a landslide national election after Hatoyama Yukio promised to relocate the Futenma base in Okinawa. Hatoyama was soon engulfed in the drama of a campaign finance scandal shortly after his election, leaving the DPJ with less room to maneuver to fulfill these campaign promises. After realizing there was no workable plan to move the base, and fearing a loss in the 2010 upper house elections as a result, Hatoyama resigned from his position as prime minister after withdrawing his campaign promise. His resignation came with an apology to local officials and to Okinawans protesting the base, saying it needed to remain in Okinawa to maintain the US-Japan alliance.

Local elections can also serve as an important barometer for upcoming national elections. In 2007, the DPJ first made gains in local elections before winning a surprise majority in Upper House elections later in the year, removing the LDP from power in the Upper House. LDP Secretary General Nakagawa Hideano resigned from his position to take the blame for the LDP's poor electoral performance, and Prime Minister Abe Shinzo resigned shortly thereafter, fearing greater loss of confidence in the LDP. Abe was much more popular in his second tenure as prime minister; in the 2015 gubernatorial elections, all ten incumbents

Regions and Prefectures of Japan

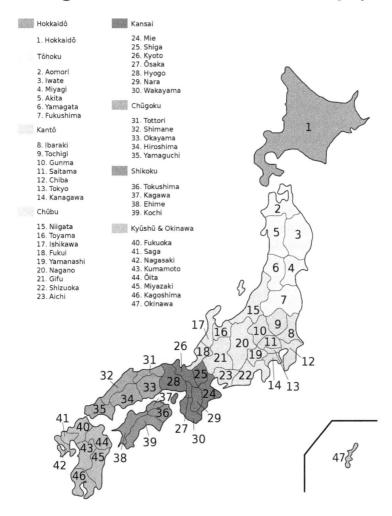

Hokkaidō	Kansai
1. Hokkaidō	24. Mie
	25. Shiga
Tōhoku	26. Kyoto
	27. Ōsaka
2. Aomori	28. Hyogo
3. Iwate	29. Nara
4. Miyagi	30. Wakayama
5. Akita	
6. Yamagata	Chūgoku
7. Fukushima	
	31. Tottori
Kantō	32. Shimane
	33. Okayama
8. Ibaraki	34. Hiroshima
9. Tochigi	35. Yamaguchi
10. Gunma	
11. Saitama	Shikoku
12. Chiba	
13. Tokyo	36. Tokushima
14. Kanagawa	37. Kagawa
	38. Ehime
Chūbu	39. Kochi
15. Niigata	Kyūshū & Okinawa
16. Toyama	
17. Ishikawa	40. Fukuoka
18. Fukui	41. Saga
19. Yamanashi	42. Nagasaki
20. Nagano	43. Kumamoto
21. Gifu	44. Ōita
22. Shizuoka	45. Miyazaki
23. Aichi	46. Kagoshima
	47. Okinawa

Figure 3.2. Regions and Prefectures of Japan. Source: https://commons.
wikimedia.org/wiki/File:Regions_and_Prefectures_of_Japan.svg.

that Abe endorsed won.[5] Local and regional elections have important implications for citizens' representation at these levels and can also have a significant impact on national and international politics.

ELECTORAL REGULATIONS

Every democratic system has procedural rules that attempt to provide as free and fair elections as possible, but these regulations are stricter and more limiting in Japan than almost anywhere else. Japan has universal voting rights in a noncompulsory system, though voters must be eighteen years of age (which was reduced from twenty in 2016). Voting rights are only for Japanese citizens, a requirement that excludes foreign nationals or permanent residents regardless of how long they may have lived in Japan. Japan does not allow dual citizenship, and the process to gain citizenship is lengthy and requires enormous documentation, compounding this voting exclusion.

For candidates and parties, regulations are also strict. Under the Public Office Election Act, Lower House campaign periods can only last twelve days, and Upper House elections cannot be more than seventeen. Candidates cannot buy advertising time on television, radio, or social media; instead, all candidates are given free space in newspapers and equal time to advertise on public media outlets. The Political Funds Control Act also heavily regulates campaign financing by stipulating that corporations, industry organizations, and unions can only donate to political parties and their fund-managing organizations, not to specific politicians or candidates. Regulations limit the monetary amount of both these donations and donations from individuals. The Political Parties Subsidies Act provides subsidies to political parties based on the number of seats each party has in the House of Representatives and the House of Councillors, as well as the proportion of votes they earned in past elections. Candidates can use these subsidies in addition to money they raise from individual donations, though there are limits to total campaign costs. Candidates are also prohibited from campaigning door to door—a common practice elsewhere—though that does not prevent them from stationing themselves outside of subway stations or apartment complexes with a sandwich board and a microphone or driving around in vans covered with posters of their faces.

These restrictions intend to ensure no party or candidate is advantaged simply because they have more money to spend in an election, but numerous regulations mean candidates and parties are often searching for loopholes just to be able to do what is considered normal in other countries. Arguments for election law reform also say such restrictive laws prevent candidates from reaching a broad audience with their message, leaving voters less educated when they go to the polls. The limited campaign window also reinforces factional politics since newer, less well-known candidates have to rely on senior party members to promote their candidacy. Further arguments point out that, even with these restrictions, campaigns in Japan remain expensive. These arguments for reform are countered

Figure 3.3. Campaign bus of Nagashima Akihisa, DPJ candidate for the 2005 Lower House election. Source: https://commons.wikimedia.org/ wiki/File:Japan_election_2005_dpj_bus.jpg.

by the fear that allowing more freedom would advantage wealthy candidates at all levels, and reform opponents often point to the United States as an example where complete campaign freedom can result in prioritizing image over substance, and in problematic campaign contributions from industries and corporations.

Voting and Running for Office

Perhaps the most obvious way people participate in politics is by voting, and eligible voter turnout rates in Japan are comparable to those in other democratic states around the world. Between 1946 and 1993, for example, voter turnout rates for general elections in Japan ranged from 64 to 77 percent. In the United Kingdom, another parliamentary system, during the same period, rates ranged from 72 to 84 percent turnout in general elections.[6] Lower turnout in the 1996 Japanese general election, the first following electoral reforms, was the result of factors unique to that election (candidates switching parties, general new procedural confusion) and of a long-term trend since the late 1950s.[7] Voter turnout for the general election in October 2021 for the Lower House was 55.93 percent, the third-lowest turnout in the postwar era. This confirms a trend in the last four general elections, where turnout has failed to reach 60 percent.

A low birth rate and longer life expectancy mean that a quarter of Japan's population is over the age of sixty-five, a phenomenon sometimes called the "graying" of society. Just as members of this age group tend to participate in NHAs more frequently than young people, they also vote more consistently as well. In the 2014 election for the House of Representatives, for example, 68 percent of citizens in their sixties went to the polls compared to 32 percent of those in their twenties. While it is more likely that senior voters are retired and have more time to spend on political participation than younger people, they might also feel more personally and immediately affected by the issues on which they are voting. Changes to social security and other forms of welfare spending, for example, would have a profound effect on seniors' quality of life.

In an effort to combat political apathy, especially among young people, the Diet voted to lower the voting age from twenty to eighteen for general elections in 2015 and for referendums in 2018. The government also created an initiative to enhance civic education in schools and to support young people in exercising their newfound civic duties. According to a Ministry of Education survey, by 2015, 94.4 percent of schools offered political education, ranging from the discussion of political activities to voting simulations.[8] Prior to the 2016 general election, the government also enlisted popular figures, like the group AKB-48, to promote voting among young people. Data from the 2016 general election reveals the turnout of eighteen-year-olds (51.7 percent) was just higher than that for forty- to forty-four-year-olds (50.3 percent) and well above those in the twenty to twenty-four age bracket (33.2 percent).

Democracies need voters, but they also need people who are willing to compete for office. Though we often associate lines of succession with monarchies or other forms of authoritarian rule (like the Kim family dynasty in North Korea) hereditary politics exists in democratic regimes too. In the early 1990s, about 45 percent of politicians in the Diet inherited their seat; even today, roughly 40 percent of LDP parliamentarians come from political families.[9] Former Prime Minister Abe Shinzo's grandfather was Kishi Nobusuke, who served as prime minister in the 1950s, and his father, Abe Shintaro, was foreign minister in the 1980s. There are numerous examples of these kinds of family connections in Japanese politics, and the phenomenon shows no evidence of abating. Koizumi Shinjiro, son of former Prime Minister Koizumi Junichiro, is expected to rise to the position of prime minister in the coming years. These hereditary lines continue in part due to the local support groups, or koenkai, which favor political families and mobilize votes in their favor, leaving little room for new or less well-connected candidates to enter or win political races. Factions also support and perpetuate family politics, especially in the LDP. Both Abe Shintaro and Abe Shinzo have headed the largest faction in the LDP where Abe's brother, Defense Minister Kishi Nobuo, is also a member. It is informally known as the "Abe faction," and many members say they can trace their factional lineage back to the "Abe line."

Just as women are underrepresented in the upper levels of bureaucracy, their numbers in government are similarly small. A woman's right to vote and run for office was first legally recognized under the postwar constitution, but it took until 2009 for the Diet to reach a high of 11.3 percent female members. In fact, Japan has the lowest participation of women in elected government positions among the thirty-eight members of the OECD. In 2021, forty-seven of the 417 members of the Diet were women—about 11 percent. For comparison, in 2021, women held 31 percent of seats in the US Congress, 34 percent of seats in the United Kingdom's Parliament, and 31 percent of seats in Germany's national Parliament, the Bundestag. One of the policies of the 2012 Abe administration was to increase the percentage of women in all sectors, not just politics, and a 2020 cabinet decision set a goal to have 35 percent of women candidates in national elections.

Some countries, like Belgium, have had success at increasing women's participation in politics by instituting gender quota systems that require a certain percentage of candidates on a party's ballot to be women. In Japan's case, legislation has been less effective because political parties are simply urged to make the number of male and female candidates as equal as possible and are encouraged to set targets for gender parity. The law includes no penalties for parties that fail to do so, nor does it include incentives for encouragement. It can also be difficult to recruit women to run for office in Japan, though the number of women in local politics does tend to be higher than in national politics. Some point to the persistence of a paternalistic social structure and attitudes toward women's roles as explanations for political underrepresentation. Others point to institutional explanations, such as the lack of effective legislation, or the power of established support groups that favor one candidate or family. There are women who hold powerful political positions in Japan, such as Koike Yuriko, governor of Tokyo, or Takaichi Sanae, an LDP Lower House representative who has held various cabinet positions.

The July 2022 Upper House election saw a record high of 33.2 percent women among the candidates, and more than half of the Constitutional Democratic Party and the Japan Communist Party's candidates were women. While the LDP increased the number of female candidates for this election, women still only made up 23.3 percent of the total LDP candidates. Of the 181 female candidates in this race, thirty-five won seats—twenty-one from electoral districts and fourteen from PR—a record-breaking step forward for women in politics. Even with these wins, the Diet still holds less than 10 percent female lawmakers, illustrating that Japan has to work harder to promote gender parity in politics.

CRITIQUES OF THE PARTY SYSTEM

Even with factional competition, many pundits and scholars interested in politics wonder how a governing body dominated by one party for so long could function democratically. Would Japan not be better served with a two-party system, where there are two competitive, dominant parties with diverging platforms and

Figure 3.4. Koike Yuriko, Tokyo's governor from 2016 to the present. Source: https://commons.wikimedia.org/wiki/File:Yuriko_Koike_2016.jpg.

ideologies, such as in the US? Or would Japan benefit more from a multiparty system, where candidates from more than two parties run for elections and all have the capacity to gain control of legislatures, separately or in coalitions, such as in Germany? These questions have plagued Japanese politics for decades, ever since center, right, and far-right parties joined to defeat the Socialist left parties in the 1950s, thus creating the system of one-party dominance. The reality is that each type of system has its advantages and disadvantages. Two-party systems can lead to stability in government, with regular changes of parties in power, but they can also limit voter choice and polarize populations along party lines. Multiparty systems might give voters more choices and they might better represent minority opinions, but coalition governments that compromise to produce significant public policy can be difficult to form. A system of one-party dominance, which is found in Japan but also in Sweden, Italy, and Israel, also has its trade-offs. A government that anticipates holding on to power might be better able to implement policies that address long-term problems like climate change, but legislators in other systems may not plan past the next election cycle. On the other hand, longevity in office can also breed complacency and corruption.

Many who closely follow Japanese politics thought that the 1994 electoral reform would finally bring about the much-discussed two-party system in Japan; it was not until 2009 that an opposition party, the Democratic Party of Japan, would win the government. Once in office, however, the DPJ did not offer policies that differed significantly from those of the LDP, and the party's mishandling of the 2011 Triple Disaster, plus its generally weak performance, brought the LDP back to power in 2012.[10] This suggests that merely alternating power among parties does not necessarily produce positive outcomes. Until opposition parties can articulate policies and ideologies that are distinct from the LDP, and until they can better organize themselves to capitalize on voter apathy and voter dissatisfaction with the LDP, it's likely the current system of one-party dominance will continue.

4

THE BUREAUCRACY

Where does real power reside in the Japanese state? So far, we've learned about emperors with largely symbolic roles, an elected Diet that checks the powers of the prime minster and executive branch, a judicial system that lacks the will to check the powers of the Diet, and an institutionalized party system that one party has mostly dominated for decades. To gain a holistic view of Japanese government, it is critical to consider Japan's bureaucrats and their role in governing and policymaking.

The term "bureaucracy" may conjure images of red tape, endless forms, and paper pushing, but every democracy—and other kinds of government as well—needs a highly skilled group of civil servants. One of the most influential theorists of modern Western society, Max Weber, believed that bureaucracy functions as an organizational structure that promotes norms and efficient practices and is therefore essential for the continuance of democracy itself.[1] Many observers of Japanese politics emphasize the major part bureaucracy plays in the national governance of Japan. Political scientist Chalmers Johnson, for instance, wrote that highly competitive ministries rule Japan, and politicians merely act as a safety valve in case of bureaucratic overreach.[2] Bureaucrat-politician competition is not unique to Japan; in fact, a distinguishing feature of many parliamentary systems, and the US federal system with the growth of the "administrative state," is the power exercised by bureaucracy in shaping public policy. As many attempts at bureaucratic reform can attest, there is no simple answer to balancing bureaucratic and politician power.

From the beginning of the Shōwa era, power rested with three groups in Japan—the militarists and their civilian supporters, the *zaibatsu* (large industrial and banking conglomerates), and the bureaucracy. These three groups made and executed major decisions in both domestic and foreign policy.[3] Postwar reforms moved quickly toward demilitarization, barring politicians perceived as too close to the militarists from running for office and dismantling the zaibatsu. In contrast, no Allied policy identified the bureaucracy as a target for reform. As a practical matter, the Allies knew that they could not supply the necessary number of trained personnel to govern Japan effectively after surrender and that leaving the administrative structure intact would be in their best interest. In this way, Japan's bureaucracies largely survived postwar reforms.

THE MINISTRY OF INTERNATIONAL TRADE AND INDUSTRY

During the following decades of uninterrupted LDP rule, administrative reforms aimed at strengthening the power of the cabinet and its ministers allowed bureaucracies to take an increasingly active role in policymaking. One of the most powerful bureaucracies during this time was the Ministry of International Trade and Industry (MITI),[4] which played a large role in the country's postwar economic recovery. MITI targeted specific industries for development, protected young and promising infant industries from international competition, and helped Japan gain a competitive advantage in trade with other countries. This may sound familiar to the state-assisted capitalism developed during the Meiji era. The active role MITI took in economic planning sometimes became a source of conflict with other countries, especially the United States, as some elected and appointed officials argued this government intervention gave Japan an unfair advantage over other countries in trade. Even so, MITI was not infallible. One of its most notorious missteps was the assumption that Japanese cars wouldn't sell in the American market. Honda Soichiro, of the Honda Motor Company, defied MITI's efforts to block the exportation of Japanese autos and went on to become the number one seller of motorcycles in the US and, by the 1970s, a significant supplier of passenger vehicles too. Honda was also a fierce opponent of placing import tariffs on foreign goods, a policy that was popular with many industrial associations at the time, because he thought the tariffs would have a reciprocal effect on Japanese exports.[5] Despite missteps, Japan experienced massive economic growth throughout the 1950s and 1960s, due at least in part to the guidance of MITI. By 1968, Japanese GDP was second only to the United States. In the 1980s, Japanese banks were among the most powerful in the world, investing heavily in the United States and elsewhere and enjoying the pinnacle of Japanese economic growth

THE MINISTRY OF FINANCE

If MITI was praised for its role in economic growth, the Ministry of Finance (MOF), another powerful bureaucratic agency, was blamed for policies that initiated the economic crisis and the subsequent stagnation of the 1990s. Following pressure from the Plaza Accords in 1985, Japan (along with France, West Germany, and the United Kingdom) agreed to increase the value of its artificially low currency relative to the US dollar. This was part of an effort to give foreign companies access to Japanese markets by making foreign products more affordable for Japanese consumers. Prior to the 1980s, banks were tightly regulated by the MOF. This left little incentive for innovation, but as long as banks were protected by the MOF, they were assured a profit margin and protection from bankruptcy. When the

MOF began to move away from this regulation and protection regime, banks were left to find their own borrowers and projects, even while they lacked the ability to correctly evaluate borrowers. Their overlending created an asset price bubble, particularly in the stock market and in housing; in the late 1980s, the value of downtown commercial property in Tokyo, already the world's most expensive property, saw a tenfold increase between 1985 and 1989.[6] This, combined with a Bank of Japan monetary policy to lower interest rates in the face of a devalued currency—for too much and for too long—flooded the market with easy money and credit. When asset prices began to decline in the early 1990s, banks found themselves with massive debt and loan defaults as various financial institutions couldn't pay back what they had borrowed.

Asset prices had collapsed by 1992, but poor recovery policies meant the economic stagnation continued through the 1990s, earning the era the nickname of the "Lost Decade." Consumer confidence plunged and consumption decreased, leading to a long period of deflation. The real estate market was also hit hard; in Tokyo, housing prices did not rise again until 2007. Many banking and financial companies closed their doors for good. Ineffective recovery policies failed to stimulate the economy, and by the end of the 1990s, Japan was still facing major economic difficulties with increasing bankruptcies, growing unemployment, and a fragile financial system. The economic crisis also uncovered rampant corruption at all levels of Japanese business, bureaucracy, and politics. The Recruit Scandal, so named because of the human resources company Recruit, uncovered insider trading practices that initially involved seventeen Diet leaders from multiple parties. It was later found that up to thirty members of the Diet had benefitted financially from insider trading, including former Prime Minister Nakasone Yasuhiro and then-Prime Minister Takeshita Noboru who, along with his cabinet, were forced to resign. The shame of this scandal, combined with continued economic stagnation, contributed to a loss of confidence in the LDP (even though all parties had someone involved) and their loss of power in 1993.

The Ministry of Finance's mishandling of the economic crisis of the 1980s and 1990s, combined with several corruption scandals in different ministries, brought the bureaucracy harsh criticism. One of the sources of bureaucratic power is the social prestige attached to civil service. Bureaucrats are commonly chosen from among the best and the brightest who have passed rigorous schooling, training, and tests to prepare for their careers in government. There is a high morale and mutual trust among bureaucrats because they have so many things in common; many come from families with ties that go back generations, and many graduate from the same departments and colleges known to produce future government officials (Tokyo and Kyoto Universities provide about half the candidates who pass the Higher Civil Service Examinations).[7] A shared sense of duty also binds bureaucrats to serve the nation in a revered profession going back to the Meiji period. While Japanese society had come to tolerate and even expect a certain level of corruption among politicians, the image of the infallible bureaucrat emerged from the 1990s heavily tarnished. In recent years, civil service has

Figure 4.1. The Tokyo University entrance exam results on display on March 10, 2007. With Tokyo University being one of the most prestigious universities, passing these exams is a major step in one's personal life and career, and many aspiring civil servants are educated at Tokyo and Kyoto Universities. By tradition, new students are cheered on by current students and are thrown in the air. Source: https://commons.wikimedia.org/wiki/File:Tokyo_University_Entrance_Exam_Results_4.JPG

been recruiting fewer top graduates from these elite universities for government work. As the Japanese economy matured and became more complex, the need for an elite bureaucracy to spearhead modernization declined. At the same time, private sector employment offered higher paying opportunities for the "best and brightest," making civil service a less attractive option.[8] By the recruitment cycle of 2022, the number of applicants for the civil service exam had plunged 60 percent from peak levels in 1996.

Regardless of past scandals and mismanagements, employment in a government ministry is still a selective and, therefore, high-status occupation in Japan. Only about 9 percent of ministerial hopefuls pass the Higher Civil Service Examinations.[9] This narrow base of recruitment means it has been difficult for women to enter ministerial work in equal numbers as men. This gendered discrepancy is especially stark in the upper levels of administrative machinery. In 2014, Prime Minister Abe's government launched a new system to manage personnel appointments that gave greater power to the prime minister's office to make key decisions in the promotion and transfer of high-ranking bureaucrats. Those who praised the initiative hoped it would increase the number of women in key positions of government, while critics warned it would invite favoritism into the promotion process. In May 2020, Japan's Cabinet Bureau for Personal Affairs reported an all-time hiring high of 36.8 percent women into new civil service positions, yet women remain grossly underrepresented in elite bureaucratic positions.

In many places, interpersonal connections between business, politics, and bureaucracy are important. In Japan, a practice of rotating officials among these different sectors maintains these important connections. This practice is *amakudari,* which means "descent from heaven." As a bureaucrat rises through the ranks of their ministry, the ladder narrows to fewer and fewer top positions. With the appointment of a new administrative vice minister, the highest position except for the top minister, everyone who entered the ministry around the same time of the new vice minister is expected to retire. This feudal custom continues so that the authority and seniority of the new vice minister is preserved. Officials can then "parachute" down from the heaven of ministerial work into a prestigious position with a private business, financial institution, or other organization closely linked to the government. A similar, heavily criticized practice, known as the "revolving door," exists in the US. Proponents of this practice say it rewards officials for their years of service and hard work. Critics maintain this practice encourages corrupt practices, such as contract bid rigging and slack supervision of industry, which is also known as regulatory capture. After the 2011 Fukushima nuclear disaster, many pointed to the high numbers of amakudari officials at both the Tokyo Electric Power Company and at the Nuclear Regulatory Authority as evidence that the revolving door between government and industry can lead to disastrous consequences.

Governmental transparency is key to a functioning democracy, though no country is completely free of corruption. The nongovernmental organization Transparency International compiles the Corruption Perceptions Index (CPI), a tool that attempts to recognize, compare, and report public sector corruption in countries around the world. Measuring corruption is a difficult task because it is something most governments actively try to conceal. The CPI uses data from surveys and performance assessments collected from institutions like the African Development Bank, the World Economic Forum, and the World Bank, among others. The CPI's 2020 reports revealed that levels of corruption in Japan are comparatively quite low. Out of 180 countries worldwide, Japan ranks as the nineteenth least corrupt, performing better than the United States, which is ranked twenty-fifth. In the Asia Pacific region, where the average score out of 100 (with 100 being least corrupt) is forty-five, Japan performs significantly better with a score of seventy-four. In Japan, as in many other countries in East Asia, the line between corruption and the cultural practice of conducting business based on personal relationships and connections is blurry.

Today, the various bureaucratic arms of Japanese government continue to wield political power and can provide stability in times of frequent ministerial turnover. One of the voting issues in the 2009 general election was decreasing bureaucratic influence, yet the resignation of five prime ministers between 2006 and 2012 gave the bureaucracy the option to wait out any prime minister with whom it disagreed, all while it pursued bureaucratic policy interests. That is not to say that the bureaucracy has its own policy agenda independent of legislators or other interest groups. Extensive and time-consuming negotiations among government agencies, politicians, and relevant interest groups are common precursors to policy decisions. These negotiations are rarely visible to the public and only appear openly in the Diet or in the media when the negotiation process has failed. A memorable example is the violence that broke out among Diet lawmakers in September of 2015 during a debate about allowing the Japanese Self-Defense Forces to assist allies in overseas operations. Photos that surfaced show LDP House of Councillors member Sato Masahisa landing a punch of the chin of Democratic Party of Japan Councillor Konishi Hiroyuki. Opposition lawmakers scramble on top of one another to grab the committee chairman's microphone in an effort to prevent him from calling a vote on the bills. This kind of melee is uncommon in the usually reserved Diet, where the process of prior negotiations (called *nemawashi*) has often built consensus around a bill before it is discussed in the Diet.

It is not entirely correct to assume, as Chalmers Johnson did in 1975, that bureaucracy solely runs the political show. Often, deliberative councils draft legislation after meeting with interested parties and legislators, and the Cabinet then introduces that bill to the Diet. Many have referred to this relationship between political parties (specifically the LDP), big business, and bureaucracy as the "Iron Triangle" or "Japan, Inc.," but the balance of power among these three actors can be uneven and is frequently shifting. There is still considerable competition between appointed bureaucrats and politicians whose need for reelection drives their policy preferences. The bureaucracy also tends to prepare bills that are favorable to the LDP, so what appears to be legislative rubber-stamping is often the bureaucracy acting in the shadow of the LDP. Furthermore, the balance of power between politicians and bureaucracy has shifted in favor of the prime minister as early as Nakasone and, more recently, during Koizumi's and Abe's tenures. Abe's long tenure heading the executive, various reforms aimed at regulating bureaucratic promotions and appointments, and a concentrated effort to increase the prime minister's exposure to policy expertise all point to a tip in power favoring the ruling party relative to the bureaucracy.

Powerful bureaucracies exist all over the world, both in democratic countries like France and in authoritarian countries like China. As in many other countries, a career in the civil service is highly prestigious and sought-after, though rarely is it obtained among applicants in Japan, especially among women. A well-skilled and functional bureaucracy is important for efficient day-to-day operations and can complement the legislative, executive, and judicial branches. A tension between government, various ministries, and the bureaucrats that make up their ranks is a normal and even desirable part of democratic governance in Japan and elsewhere.

5

CIVIL SOCIETY AND POLITICAL
PARTICIPATION

If one imagines the institutions of the state as a car and government as the driver, then citizens are the passengers who shout directions from the back seat. Some voices are louder than others and can more effectively persuade the driver to take the vehicle in a specific direction. Cars exist for their passengers just as democracies exist for their people. This chapter explores some of the various ways citizens in Japan can and do engage in politics.

CIVIL SOCIETY

The term "civil society" refers to the organized, nonstate, and nonmarket sector of society. Though the exact definition of what comprises civil society is debatable, we can think of it as a set of voluntary groups people join when they act in or want to influence the public interest.[1] This includes activist groups, charities, religious groups, professional associations, and sports leagues, to name a few.[2] In a democracy, civil society groups have respect for the rule of law and for free speech— that is, the ability for other groups to be able to express their opinions and preferences without fear of violence or retaliation. A diverse and active civil society is vital to democratic governance because it can both encourage political participation and act as a watchdog to limit and control the power of the state. NGOs and interest groups can promote civic education and develop programs where citizens learn how to work with each other, debate public issues, and express their opinions. Groups that bring together people who share similar interests and values can bridge racial, ethnic, or political divides and bond people in the group with shared trust, thus creating social capital.[3] Ideally, civil society can contribute to a well-functioning society and a strong democracy.

Like many other advanced, democratic societies in the world, Japan has a plethora of civil society groups that have many members and span many different areas of interest. A study conducted between 2005 and 2007 found that there were roughly 440,000 civil society organizations in Japan that had obtained corporate status or government registration.[4] Of these, religious corporations were the most popular followed by political organization, labor unions, medium and small business cooperatives, and registered nonprofit organizations.[5] The state heavily regulates and supervises many of these incorporated civil society organizations; in fact, some exist because of state initiatives and are staffed by retired bureaucrats through the process of *amakudari* (explained in chapter 4). Some of these organizations also receive state and corporate funding specifically meant to carry out state programs. The Ministry of Economy, Trade, and Industry (METI), for example, supervises the Japan Productivity Center for Socioeconomic Development, a nongovernmental organization established in 1955 by business leaders to promote industrial activity.

Regulations that govern the legal existence of civil society groups in Japan are complex, and forming an accurate picture of civil society can be difficult. Although the absence of legal status means these organizations lack legal protections and cannot rent office space or borrow money from financial institutions, they are also relatively free of government oversight. Surveys of 300,000 neighborhood associations (NHAs) have found that only 7 percent are legally recognized as community-based associations.[6] A system of compulsory grouping of families for joint civic responsibilities is a custom introduced to Japan from China in the seventh century.[7] NHAs are one of Japan's most enduring institutions, with modern versions reaching back to the Edo period, when local groups formed to prevent fires that would periodically destroy neighborhoods. Many associations formed in response to the 1923 Great Kanto earthquake, and NHAs became the main force of home front mobilization during World War II, when the government made membership compulsory. Though abolished by Allied Occupation authorities, by the late 1950s, NHAs could still be found in almost all municipalities.

Today, NHAs are local groups of about one hundred families that perform an impressive variety of functions, from overseeing the elaborate protocols for trash separation and recycling to planning local festivals. Local governmental actions can be restricted in practical and legal ways by budget deficits and Japan's unitary governmental system. When this happens, NHAs can act as a bridge between local governments and society by performing services that the government would normally provide or by conveying residents' needs to local officials. They can perform neighborhood safety patrols, distribute public health information, or conduct disaster response drills in case of earthquakes or floods. In the event of a disaster, like the 1995 Kobe earthquake, NHAs across the country can mobilize to receive victims and provide medical attention, food, and shelter. Despite their usefulness to local governments, NHAs present local challenges too. Some people see the members as busybodies with clipboards, and they feel pressured to participate due to a fear of alienation; "the nail that sticks up" will be hammered into an NHA. There is also a severe gender imbalance, where almost all NHA leadership is comprised of men, and an age imbalance, where participation is highest among seniors. A 2015 survey conducted by the Ministry of Health, Labor, and Welfare found that participation is highest among people in their sixties and seventies where, respectively, 55 percent and 64 percent of those surveyed said they participated in NHA activities at least once a month or a few times per year. Participation is lowest among people in their twenties and thirties (15 percent and 25 percent for the same questions, respectively).[8]

Compared to Japan's local civil society organizations, the number of professional civil society organizations is small, especially compared to other places; for example, the US has many large and powerful groups such as Greenpeace, the World Wildlife Federation, or the AARP. Those that do exist in Japan are usually staffed by small groups of people who work with limited and variable budgets and that have small memberships from which to raise funds. This relative weakness of professional civil society may be a result of the strict governmental regulations on nonprofit organizations, or perhaps the limited labor mobility in Japan compared to other places. Whereas it is common in the US to take a position in a low-paying nonprofit right out of college for a few years, in Japan there is a higher risk that position will involuntarily become permanent employment. Whatever the explanation, professional civil society groups have historically had little success influencing policy outcomes; most nonprofits cannot compete with the power of the bureaucracy, and campaign financing laws prevent the kind of "candidate sponsorship" that is rampant in the US.

MASS MEDIA

The political mass media have long had an important but controversial role in Japanese politics. Ideally, media should provide information to citizens they otherwise would not have access to, whether that is reporting on events that are happening or discoveries they make through investigative reporting. This can help citizens make informed and responsible civic choices. The media can function as the "eyes and ears" of the people. For this reason, the media also acts as a "watchdog" that makes sure political figures are upholding their oaths of office. *The Washington Post*'s Watergate reporting and the mass attention it brought to political crimes and misdeeds is one of the most frequently cited examples of the power of a free press. Others point to the critical programming by stations like TV Asahi as contributing to the LDP's loss of power in 1993.

Newspapers in Japan have some of the highest circulation rates in the world. For context, consider Japan's most popular newspaper, the *Yomiuri Shimbun*, which has a circulation rate of almost eight million compared to the *New York Times*' 5.4 million. Generally, Japan respects the principles of media freedom and pluralism. There are numerous national and local media outlets and one state-sponsored public media outlet, the Japan Broadcasting Company (NHK). Journalists aren't murdered or jailed, and the foreign press operates in Japan. Out of 180 countries, Japan ranks sixty-seventh in press freedom according to the 2021 report from the Reporters Without Borders World Press Freedom (WPF) Index. For comparative context, Norway ranks first, the US forty-fourth, and the People's Republic of China

Figure 5.1 Typical page one of the *Yomiuri-Shimbun*,
https://en.wikipedia.org/wiki/Yomiuri_Shimbun#/
media/File:Yomiuri-Shimbun-sample-p1.jpg.

ranks 177th. While sixty-seventh is better than average from a global perspective, a more accurate comparison would be with other democratic countries, where we would expect to see high levels of press freedom. In this case, a rank of sixty-seventh places Japan at the bottom of the list when it is compared with the other thirty-seven Organization for Economic Cooperation and Development (OECD) countries.

Japanese reporting is dominated by *kisha* (reporter "clubs"), which are exclusive groups of reporters from major Japanese newspapers that operate from political and government offices. Kisha membership allows exclusive access to politicians and their press representatives and encourages close relationships between reporters and politicians. The Japan Newspaper Publishers and Editors Association would argue kisha perform important functions. The clubs receive news quickly since they are in the same building where the action is happening. They sort through a lot of information and then release it quickly too. But while a close relationship between reporter and politician may benefit the reporter and politician, it does

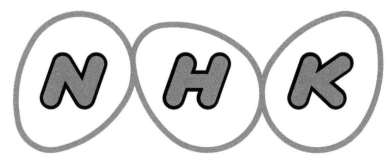

Figure 5.2. The Japan Broadcasting Company (Nippon Hyōsō Kyōkai, or NHK) logo from 1995 to 2020, https://en.wikipedia.org/wiki/NHK#/media/File:NHK_logo.svg.

not promote transparent reporting. If these relationships are built on trust, and a reporter's access to information is determined by how trustworthy they are, then hard-hitting investigative reporting is not in the reporter's best interest. When reporters simply act as a mouthpiece for politicians and even large companies, the watchdog function essentially disappears. Following the Fukushima Daiichi disaster in 2011, the Tokyo Electric Power Company (TEPCO) kisha reporters never received clear information from TEPCO leaders or from the government about unsafe radiation levels or evacuation mandates, and reporters never asked the right questions either. Members of the foreign and independent press are often barred from press conferences where there is already a kisha present (a kisha rule that gives them a monopoly over the "news") which makes information gathering and reporting that much more difficult.

Even with the controversial kisha, comparatively speaking, sixty-seventh is a good place to be; however, this still puts Japan in the "problematic" category, and Japan's ranking in the WPF Index has consistently worsened since 2013, when the Abe government passed the State Secrets Law. This law allows the government to censor or withhold sensitive documents for sixty years. Civil servants caught leaking government information can be incarcerated for ten years, while journalists or other civilians involved can face five years. Since the growth of the popularity of the nationalist right, many journalists have complained of a general climate of mistrust toward the media. While commentary and opinion reporting are slowly becoming more common, alternative forms of media like weekly magazines or online news have never really caught on with most news consumers. These factors combine to create an environment where the press is free in theory but faces many challenges to responsible reporting in practice.

CITIZEN PROTESTS

Besides participating in organized groups, activism and protest activity are also important examples of citizens' political participation. The motivations for protest activity can vary. Sometimes, protestors want a particular political outcome: for a political figure to resign or for a policy to be enacted or changed. Sometimes, protest activity can escalate into riots and explosions of frustration and anger. The Rice Riots of 1918 were the largest and most violent in Japan's history, when wartime inflation caused the price of rice and other consumer goods to skyrocket while wages remained stagnant. People were unable to afford food and other necessities. Protests that began in the countryside spread to urban areas, many rice dealers' shops were looted or burned, and tens of thousands of workers went on strike. Prime Minister Terauchi Masatake and his cabinet resigned, but conditions continued to worsen as Japan's imperial quest escalated.

Japan's relationship with the United States has been a frequent source of citizen dissent. In May and June of 1960, massive protests erupted over the passage of the revised Treaty of Mutual Cooperation and Security with the United States. These "Anpo" protests, so named for the Japanese shorthand for the security treaty, brought hundreds of thousands of people into the streets day after day, where thousands were injured and one person died. The security concerns were so great that US President Dwight D. Eisenhower's planned visit was canceled. Prime Minister Kishi Nobusuke resigned amid the protests in late June of 1960, though he continued to be active in the LDP and to influence politics from behind the scenes.

The security treaty between the US and Japan is still in effect today, a provision of which allows American military bases to operate on Japanese soil. Okinawa is host to approximately three-fourths of the 54,000 American soldiers stationed in Japan. Okinawans frequently protest the presence of these bases, citing the unfairness that such a small percentage of Japan's territory should shoulder such a large burden of hosting the military bases. There are concerns about pollution and noise that lower quality of life on the islands and harm the tourism industry. There have also been instances of violence, including charges of rape and murder, against Okinawans by American military members. Okinawans have had a difficult time trying to change national policymakers' minds about the US bases. An agreement between the US and Japan planned to relocate the existing Futenma base to an extension of the Henoko base that would be developed jointly by the US and Japan. The formal plan for the Henoko extension has existed as far back as 1999, and local opposition has existed even longer. The first municipal referendum in the city in Nago, where the extension would be located, revealed a majority of voters opposed the relocation plans. Following the vote, the mayor and municipal assembly at the time communicated the city's support to the central government and passed a resolution of acceptance. That resolution would be overturned several years later, beginning a cycle of local acceptance and opposition. In 2019, a non-legally binding prefectural referendum revealed 70 percent of voters opposed the expansion of a base at Henoko for US Marines. Conflict between the Okinawan prefectural government and the central government followed the vote because the expansion project has continued despite the referendum's results.

Figure 5.3. Masses of protestors flood the streets around Japan's national Diet building to protest the Anpo treaty with the United States, June 18, 1960, https://en.wikipedia.org/wiki/Anpo_protests#/media/File:1960_Protests_against_the_United_States-Japan_Security_Treaty_07.jpg.

There are examples where citizen protests have resulted in some success. In 1958, members of the Minamata Fishing Cooperative forced their way into the Chisso Corporation's chemical factory located in Kumamoto Prefecture. Researchers had recently discovered that the Chisso factory, since its opening in 1908, had been releasing toxic amounts of methylmercury into local waterways with their industrial wastewater. Local residents were turning up in hospitals with severe symptoms of

Figure 5.4. A crowd of Okinawans protesting the Futenma base in Ginowan, Okinawa, https://en.wikipedia.org/wiki/Protests_of_US_military_presence_in_Okinawa#/media/File:The_protesting_crowd_in_Ginowan_on_2009-11-08.jpg.

mercury poisoning (dubbed "Minamata disease"), which was eventually traced back to eating fish and shellfish caught in these contaminated waters. National and local governments agreed the Chisso factory was too economically important to shut down. When the Kumamoto prefectural government issued a partial ban on the sale of fish from the heavily polluted Minamata Bay, the Minamata and Kumamoto Prefectural fishing cooperatives demanded compensation from the Chisso Corporation. After intense media attention brought the issue of Minamata disease to the public, mediation committees formed to arbitrate an agreement between the fishing groups, the disease patients, and the Chisso Corporation. In these negotiations, the fishing groups held stronger bargaining power relative to the disease victims. The cooperatives were organized, united, legally recognized civil society groups whose industry made up a significant part of the local economy. The victims' organization, by comparison, was only recently established and weakly staffed. In 1959, the Minamata Disease Patients Families Mutual Aid Society accepted meager sums of "sympathy money" from Chisso on behalf of the disease victims. The Chisso Corporation never admitted responsibility for the mercury poisoning, and victims had to agree to seek no further compensation if it was ever proven that Chisso's wastewater was responsible for their disease. Many link the establishment of a national Environmental Agency (later the Ministry of the Environment) to the events in Minamata as Japan's attempt to bring better balance to economic development and environmental protection policies.

After Prime Minister Nakasone Yasuhiro broke up the dominant National Railway Workers' Union in 1987 (following moves similar to those of US President Ronald Reagan regarding the Air Traffic Controllers' Organization, and UK Prime Minister Margaret Thatcher's defeat of the National Union of Mineworkers), labor unions have been limited to a much smaller seat at the table. According to Nakasone's plan, this taming of the labor unions led to the collapse of the Japan Socialist Party (JSP), the leading opposition party, a decade later. Without the financial support from unions, the JSP could not compete with other parties backed by business and professional organizations.

COMMON POLITICAL ISSUES

The most pervasive political issues in Japan are not so different from those in other countries. People are concerned about the economy and employment. As in other countries, too, these issues intertwine with conversations about immigration and population decline. In 2021, Japan's childhood population hit a record low after many decades of steady decline. According to the United Nations Demographic Yearbook, the percentage of children in the overall population—11.9 percent—is the lowest ratio among thirty-three other countries with a population of over forty million. Fertility rates, which are defined as the number of children that would be born to each women if she were to live to her childbearing years and give birth to children in alignment with prevailing age-specific rates, are another way to gauge population stability. A total fertility rate of 2.1 children per women can maintain a stable population. Worldwide, fertility rates have declined since the 1970s and early 1980s, when the children of the postwar "baby boomer" generation were born. With data from the OECD, figure 5.5 demonstrates fertility rates for select OECD countries for 2020.

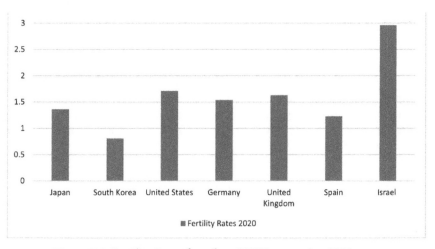

Figure 5.5. Fertility Rates for select OECD countries, 2020.

The declining fertility rate trend has accelerated particularly in East Asia in the past years, first in Japan and then in South Korea and China. Low numbers of young adults and children, combined with a postwar population boom and long average life spans can strain social spending resources as the domestic workforce shrinks. In an attempt to boost the number of workers in the economy, Japan instituted a new policy in 2017 to streamline the immigration of skilled foreign workers. The resulting influx of workers is challenging the perception of Japan as ethnically homogenous while, domestically, Japan appears to have avoided the far-right, xenophobic backlash seen in many countries in the West in recent years. Despite this policy change, problems still plague Japan's immigration system, and many criticize its conservative asylum and refugee policies. The 2021 death of Sri Lankan Wishma Sandamali after being held for over a year in a Nagoya detention facility for overstaying her visa sparked calls for reforms to Japan's deportation system. Wishma was the seventeenth detainee to die in a Japanese detention center since 2007. Japan's strict asylum regulations mean less than 1 percent of applications per year are approved compared to 30 to 40 percent in the US and in European countries.

While concerns over safety issues like homicide and mass shootings are pervasive in many countries, Japan has enjoyed relatively low comparative levels of gun-related violence. According to the World Health Organization, there were nine deaths in Japan resulting from firearms use in 2018. According to the Center for Disease Control, the number in the US for the same year was 39,740. These low figures are partly attributable to some of the strictest gun control laws in the world, which require gun owners to undergo a thirteen-step licensing process every three years that includes, among other things, a thorough background check, a mental health evaluation, and registration with a hunting organization. When Abe Shinzō was assassinated in July of 2022, the weapon used by Tetsuya Yamagami was a homemade shotgun held together with tape. Police officers have access to handguns but rarely use them in the line of duty, so police homicides and brutality are less visible as political issues. Even so, in 2020, following the Black Lives Matter protests in the US and around the world, demonstrators gathered in Tokyo to protest police brutality against underrepresented minority groups in Japan and to show solidarity with the global BLM movement. Japan has not been immune from acts of domestic terrorism, which include the 1995 sarin gas attacks in the Tokyo subway by the religious group Aum Shrinyiko. Violent acts still take place, but they are more likely to be arson or knife-related attacks than violence perpetrated with firearms.

In addition to economic and safety concerns, Japanese citizens share interests in social issues. For years, activists have pressed the Diet to introduce nondiscrimination legislation to protect what they believe to be a violation of the rights of gay, lesbian, bisexual, and transgender (LGBT) people. Same-sex marriage is banned in Japan according to Article 24 of the constitution, which defines marriage as based on the "mutual consent of both sexes," interpreted as between a man and a woman. In early 2021, however, a Sapporo court ruled the government's ban on same-sex unconstitutional, which might pave the way for future changes in the definition of marriage in Japan. Minority groups such as Japan's indigenous Ainu population have also struggled for political recognition and legal protections. In 2019, the Japanese government officially recognized the Ainu as Indigenous people, a move that requires the government to take measures to ban discrimination against them. The Ainu Promotion Act also obligates the government to facilitate people's understanding of the traditions of the Ainu and the importance of the diversity that ethnic groups contribute to society. The recently finished Upopoy Museum (officially named the Symbolic Space for Ethnic Harmony) in Hokkaido is one example meant to spread awareness and education on Ainu traditions and culture. Though some progress has been made for Ainu, other ethnic or racial minority groups, including Koreans or racially mixed individuals, continue to regularly face discrimination.

In the absence of real political competition, many in Japan who want to make real societal contributions are doing so from outside the institutionalized political system. When the average lawmaker in Japan is fifty-five, and when only 9.7 percent of the national legislature is female, as a young person, one is unlikely to see their cohort's interests clearly represented. No one younger than thirty years old remembers a time before economic stagnation, nor do they remember the hardships faced in the years following World War II, when Japan rebuilt itself into a prosperous nation. That reality has manifested in at least two political realities. First, young people seem to support the conservative LDP compared to other parties, not because they are drawn enthusiastically to the LDP's platform but because the LDP represents stability and predictability in anxious times. Polls regularly show people in their twenties and thirties approve of the LDP at higher rates than people in their sixties and older. The nationalist rhetoric of the LDP, which moved even further right under the tenure of Abe, does not seem to resonate with young people in the same way it does for older people with longer memories. At the same time, it also seems that young people are increasingly less active in traditional politics than their parents and grandparents were. As discussed earlier, voting rates are low among young people, there are few candidates younger than forty running for office, and fewer people are entering government jobs. Protest activity is limited, and even the largest protests in 2014 over the Abe security legislation had little effect on policy outcomes. That does not mean that young people are apolitical, but it does mean they may increasingly look beyond the halls of government buildings to civil society to engage in political activity.

6

DEFENSE AND FOREIGN RELATIONS

For many years, Japan's foreign policies were shaped by its interest in "catching up" to the West. Concurrent to the desire to gain equal footing with world powers is Japan's policy of forming alliances with world powers, such as the Anglo-Japan Treaty of 1902, the Tripartite Pact with Germany and Italy in 1940, and the country's postwar relationship with the US. In the late 1800s and early 1900s, this interest manifested in a series of territorial annexations (the Ryukyu Kingdom in 1879) and wars, first with China from 1894 to 1895, then by participating in the Boxer Rebellion in 1900, and then in conflict with Russia from 1904 to 1905. These modest military successes further encouraged Japan to continue its expansionist policies, eventually building an empire that spanned from the Kuril Islands and Manchuria in the north to modern-day Myanmar in South Asia and across Southeast Asia and into the Pacific. Japan joined the side of the Allied powers in World War I and was the only non-Western nation considered a "great power" to attend the 1919 signing of the Treaty of Versailles. Domestic opinion toward joining the League of Nations, however, was divided; while some in Japan thought the nation could only benefit from closer ties with Western nations like the United States and Great Britain, others thought the League was devised by Western countries with only their own benefit in mind. To assuage these doubts, the Japanese delegation proposed a Racial Equality Clause be included in the League's covenant, an addition stating the equality of all nations was a basic principle of the League. The Racial Equality Clause failed to gain traction with potential League members, not least because of its implications for the Western-dominated system characterized by colonial rule over nonwhite peoples. The rejection of the clause fueled nationalist sentiment in Japan and foreshadowed the conflicts to come in the Second World War. Though this incident with the League of Nations occurred over a century ago, a similar tension toward Japan's place in the world order still colors aspects of Japanese foreign relations today, especially with the United States and regional neighbors, though we also can see Japan act as a leader and ally in East Asia in its own right.

US-Japan Mutual Security Treaty

Signed alongside the San Francisco Peace Treaty in 1951, the US-Japan Mutual Security Treaty (or the Anpo treaty, which is shorthand for the Japanese name) was a ten-year, renewable agreement that outlined how US forces would continue to stay in Japan after the country regained sovereignty. The security treaty dovetailed with the Yoshida Doctrine, named after the postwar prime minister Yoshida Shigeru, which saw Japan relying on the US for military protection while focusing other national resources on economic recovery. Washington saw Japan as a key Cold War ally, especially in East Asia, which at the time was a region characterized by a fractured Korean peninsula, a newly Communist China, and a Soviet Union that was expanding in its breadth and capabilities. By the late 1940s, the policy was to "reverse course" on many of the reforms put into place during the early days of the occupation in response to the perceived Cold War threat in East Asia. It was against this backdrop that, despite the pacifist constitution and the postwar occupation goal of demilitarization, Yoshida's government created the Self-Defense Forces (SDF) in 1954. As Japan's economy grew, the US relied on its East Asian ally to provide economic stability to the Cold War alliance system as Japan simultaneously benefited from the same security framework.

In 1960, the security treaty was revised to grant the US the right to establish bases on Japanese soil in exchange for its pledge to defend Japan in the event of an attack. Today, there are more than eighty US military facilities spread across Japan, and more US service members are stationed there than in any other country. There have been continued controversies over the use of the bases for American operations that are not perceived to be tied to Japanese foreign policies or goals. For example, in the late 1960s, Prime Minister Sato Eisaku established principles of nonproliferation—no production, no possession, no introduction—in response to fears that US nuclear weapons housed on the bases would provoke attack and undermine the deterrent force of the US nuclear umbrella. There was also public concern when the US used the bases to support combat operations during the Vietnam War. Chapter 5 discusses other controversies associated with the American bases in Japan, especially in Okinawa, where one-third of all American service members are stationed on less than 1 percent of Japanese territory.

Recent collaborations between the US and Japanese governments have moved forward the construction of a new Marine base in Guam, a US territory, which would host many US service members relocated from Japan. The greatest stumbling block for the completion of the base in Guam is also one of the most common sticking points of the security treaty in general: who pays? Under the provisions of the security treaty, Japan shoulders most of the cost for hosting about 55,000 military personnel. Even so, Japan's yearly defense budgets tend to be below the 2 percent of GDP the US prefers its allies to spend on defense, and treaty cost-sharing is a frequently negotiated issue. Regardless, the security treaty between the US and Japan is the longest-standing agreement of its kind in the past 350 years.

Figure 6.1. Map of major US military bases in Japan.
Source: https://commons.wikimedia.org/wiki/File:Major_
US_military_bases_in_Japan.svg.

THE MINISTRIES OF DEFENSE AND FOREIGN AFFAIRS

The day-to-day responsibilities of maintaining the US-Japan relationship and of conducting Japanese foreign policy, in general, is institutionalized in a variety of different bureaucracies and organizations. On the civilian side, the Ministry of Foreign Affairs (MOFA) is the diplomatic arm of Japanese foreign relations and is made up of a variety of regional and topical bureaus, with the North American Affairs Bureau playing a primary role in shaping security and defense policy. For many years, MOFA enjoyed an elevated status relative to the Japan Defense Agency (JDA). In 2007, the JDA's profile in the defense establishment was elevated to become the Ministry of Defense (MOD), a move tied to the deepening of the US-Japan alliance, a changing security environment in East Asia and beyond, and the more frequent activities of the SDF. As a supervisory institution for the SDF, the MOD has therefore taken on an increasingly important role in security policymaking, and in 2021, the MOD asked for a budgetary spending increase that would entail the largest percentage jump in eight years.

Defense spending is a significant component of many countries' foreign relations, and it offers clues into how a country views its security. Increases in defense spending, for example, may signal that a country feels threatened or is planning a future operation. In Japan, the defense budget funds the maintenance of the SDF as well as responsibilities under the US security treaty. The SDF consists of the Ground, Maritime, and Air Self-Defense Forces, and the prime minister serves as commander in chief.[1] Readers might remember that the postwar constitution renounced war as a legitimate means for solving international disputes (Section 1 of Article 9) and held that Japan would therefore not maintain land, sea, or air forces or any other kind of war potential (Section 2). Article 9, which was included when demilitarization was still a policy of the occupation, was subsequently interpreted to mean that the constitution does not deny Japan the right to self-defense; therefore, according to this interpretation, the SDF was not in violation of Article 9. Between 1976 and 1987, amid a policy environment of anti-war sentiment and economic recovery imperatives, Japan stuck to a self-imposed limit to spend less than 1 percent of its GDP on defense. Even after breaking the 1 percent ceiling in 1987 under the more "hawkish" or aggressive defense leadership of Prime Minister Nakasone Yasuhiro, Japanese defense spending still hovered just above the 1 percent mark, a comparatively low figure. A record-high defense budget passed in November of 2021, for example, will bring the annual total defense spending to 1.14 percent of GDP. To put this into perspective, the United States spends about 3 percent of its GDP on defense, and South Korea spends approximately 2.5 percent.

But 1.14 percent of the third-largest GDP in the world is still a large figure, and Japan has, by many measures, a well-equipped military force. In 2020, the Lowy Institute's Asia Power Index ranked Japan seventh out of twenty-six countries in Asia in terms of its military capability.[2] This sub-indicator of "military capability" attempts to measure conventional military power by assessing military spending, total active forces, weapons and capabilities, and military posture in the region. A second sub-indicator, "defense networks," attempts to measure number, depth, and combined strength of regional alliances. In this measure, Japan scored third after the US and Australia, both Japanese allies. The Asia Power Index places Japan third out of twenty-six countries in overall composite power scores, after the US and China.

Despite its capability, the practical use of the SDF has been constrained and controversial because Japanese foreign policy involving the use of the SDF walks a fine line of constitutional permissibility. In 1991, the US called on Japan to participate in a coalition of forces operating under the United Nations mandate to remove Iraqi forces from Kuwait. In what many in Japan saw as a notoriously embarrassing misstep, Tokyo only agreed to send monetary aid to the efforts but not to commit military resources. This "checkbook diplomacy" brought criticism from Washington and prompted then US Secretary of State James Baker to publicly urge Japan to take a more active role in international diplomacy and to assume broader responsibilities for international stability. The implication of the statement was that the US would be dissatisfied with a Japan that offered economic aid but tried to stay out of political controversy. Many changes quickly followed. In 1992, the government enacted a law that allowed the SDF to dispatch troops overseas to support United Nations peacekeeping missions. Since then, the SDF has participated in nine missions, including in Cambodia, Mozambique, and Zaire.

An often overlooked stipulation of the 1992 law also allows SDF forces to deploy to peacekeeping missions that are not under the mandate of the UN, but it was not until 2019 that two SDF officers would be sent to the Sinai Peninsula to serve under the Multinational Force and Observers (MFO) there. After the US launched the War on Terror following the 9/11 terrorist attacks, activities by the SDF expanded to cover areas such as the Indian Ocean and the Middle East. US President George W. Bush and Japanese Prime Minister Koizumi Junichiro seemed to have a close relationship, one through which President Bush sought Japanese assistance with Operation Enduring Freedom in Afghanistan. In October of 2001, the Diet enacted a special law dispatching Maritime Self-Defense Forces to refuel American, British, and French warships in the Indian Ocean. From 2004 to 2006, following the US-led invasion of Iraq, the 5,500- member Japanese Iraq Reconstruction and Support Group was stationed in southern Iraq to provide humanitarian assistance in noncombat zones. This doubling down on the US alliance has not come without its costs, both monetary and human, including the fatal shooting of two Japanese diplomats in Iraq in 2003, the kidnapping of Japanese aid workers and journalists in 2004, and the beheading of Kenji Goto, a Japanese video journalist, by the Islamic State of Iraq and Syria (ISIS) in 2015. Many in Japan remain wary of the alliance with the US and fear America's deep and wide involvement in international affairs will draw Japan into unnecessary conflicts. On the other hand, many remain convinced that, despite potential costs, a strong relationship with the United States is Japan's best bet at security in an evolving East Asia.

While past interpretations of Article 9 have allowed for self-defense, more recent interpretive efforts have been in favor of collective defense, or of allowing Japan to militarily assist an ally if that ally is attacked by a third party. All sovereign states possess the right to enter into collective defense agreements; the North Atlantic Treaty Organization (NATO), established in 1949, for example, is one of the longest-standing collective defense agreements. Japan's ability to engage in collective defense was limited by interpretations of Article 9 that prohibited a military response unless there was clear evidence of some threat to the homeland. In 2014, an advisory panel formed by then Prime Minister Abe recommended Article 9 be reinterpreted to allow for a wider use of military power. Abe originally lobbied for a reinterpretation that allowed for collective defense, but there was fierce opposition from lawmakers and citizens. The final legislation Abe and the LDP would promote in 2015 allowed for collective self-defense, meaning Japan could militarily come to the aid of its allies but only in situations where there is evidence of a material threat posed to Japanese interests and only as a means of

Figure 6. 2. Japanese Prime Minister Koizumi Junichiro shakes hands with US President George W. Bush in the White House Rose Garden on September 25, 2001. Source: https://commons.wikimedia.org/wiki/File:President_George_W._Bush_and_Prime_Minister_Junichiro_Koizumi_of_Japan_Shake_Hands.jpg.

last resort and with limited force. After a drawn-out and dramatic vote, which involved various attempts at filibustering and a fist fight on the usually staid Diet floor, the "Peace and Security Preservation Legislation" passed both houses of the Diet and came into effect in 2016.

While the US has welcomed many of these reforms, a more muscular defense policy has not been as equally well received by Japan's East Asian neighbors, especially by China. Japanese diplomats have publicly repeated that the US-Japan alliance does not target any third parties, yet Chinese leaders have voiced their concerns over what they allege as efforts to contain an increasingly powerful China. In 2017, Japan joined countries across East Asia and North and South America in the Trans-Pacific Partnership (TPP), a regional trade organization that conspicuously does not include China among its members.[3] Under the leadership of Abe Shinzo, the Quadrilateral Security Dialogue was also resurrected, and though it is not a formal security alliance, it has become increasingly active in bringing together Japan, the US, Australia, and India to tackle issues related to security, the economy, and health. For Japan, "the Quad" is key to its foreign policy goal of a "Free and Open Indo-Pacific," an umbrella term that encompasses the promotion of maritime cooperation and enforcement, free trade, and stability in the Indo-Pacific region. The Quad coalition has bonded over a mutual concern of what these nations see as China's increasingly aggressive behavior in the region

Figure 6.3. Government leaders from the Quad states, who held the first in-person Quad meeting in Washington, DC, in 2021. From left to right: Japanese Prime Minister Yoshihide Suga, Indian Prime Minister Narendra Modi, US President Joe Biden, and Australian Prime Minister Scott Morrison. Source: https://en.wikipedia.org/wiki/Quadrilateral_Security_Dialogue#/media/File:President_Joe_Biden_with_the_Prime_Ministers_of_Australia,_India,_and_Japan.jpg.

under the leadership of Xi Jinping. Though the TPP and the Quad state that their actions are only meant for their own benefit and are not meant to be to the detriment of China, perceptions of security can be as important as actual security in international relations. For this reason, many states in the region—including Japan—are experiencing the dilemma of how to increase their own security without decreasing the perceived security of others.

REGIONAL RELATIONS

China-Japan relations were strained under Abe's leadership, partly because of the revisions to Japan's defense policies but also because of Abe's flirtation with historical revisionism. Abe, a member of Nippon Kaigi (the Japan Conference), a far-right nationalist nongovernmental organization and lobbying body, has been accused of promoting an alternative view of history in which Japan should be applauded for liberating East Asia from its colonial oppressors. More specifically, many members believe that the Tokyo Trials were illegitimate, the Nanjing Massacre was exaggerated, and the existence of "comfort women" is questionable. Abe promoted textbook revisions to support "patriotic education." Like former Prime Minister Koizumi and other politicians before him, Abe visited the controversial Yasukuni Shrine, which is meant to commemorate those who have died in Japanese wars, on more than one occasion. South Korea has repeatedly demanded Japan pay appropriate reparations to victims who were sexual slaves of the Japanese Imperial Army, and to Koreans who were forced into labor during wartime, though Japan says the issue was settled in 1965 when the two countries normalized relations and Japan provided more than $800 million in aid to South Korea. Yet the issue remains far from resolved and has even led to a flare-up of tensions between the two countries over a group of islands that both countries claim as their own.

Territorial disputes are not uncommon in East Asia. Japan and South Korea both claim the Takeshima Islands (or Dokdo Islands, as they are known in South Korea), Japan and China disagree over who has the legitimate right to the Senkaku Islands (known as the Daioyu Islands in China), and China has additional disputed claims with many countries in Southeast Asia over territories in the East and South China Seas. Rights to these contested territories come with access to two hundred nautical miles of Exclusive Economic Zones (EEZs) and the resources (fish, oil, gas) within them, plus the navigation of waterways and airspace. In addition to material resources, states are also unwilling to relinquish control of a territory for fear of the audience costs of looking weak or of the precedent it may set. Some territorial disputes can go on for decades—Japan and Russia still disagree over which state owns the Kuril Islands, and Russia (which was then the Soviet Union) did not sign the San Francisco Peace Treaty in 1951 because of this disagreement.

Concerns about territorial aggression extend to Taiwan and whether mainland China will attempt to unify the People's Republic of China with the democratic Republic of China. While the US government maintains a strong but unofficial relationship with Taiwan through the 1979 Taiwan Relations Act, Japan's policy toward Taiwan has been less clear. Japan recognizes the Communist government in Beijing's claim to governing legitimacy of China yet not its claim to sovereignty over Taipei. Japan has significant trading ties to Taiwan but does not sell Taipei defensive arms, unlike Washington. Japan has been a driving force behind the Quad dialogue, from which Taiwan has benefited, yet Taiwan is not an official member. Most importantly, Japan has no domestic law similar to the Taiwan Relations Act that commits support in the event of cross-strait conflict. Against this backdrop, 2021 brought much concern among scholars and policymakers that China may use its growing military power to force reunification with Taiwan, which brought much attention to Taiwan-Japan relations. Suga, the former prime minister, joined US President Joe Biden in April of 2021 in a statement that underscored the importance of peaceful cross-strait relations, deliberately using language unlikely to provoke offense. The ambiguity of Japan's Taiwan policy is strategic and mirrors similarly vague aspects of the US policy as well; both are judged to have deterrent value. Added to this is a long-term trend demonstrating an incremental deepening of ties between Japan and Taiwan and initiatives designed to bring together policymakers from the US, Taiwan, and Japan to discuss security issues. Japan's high economic dependence on China and its security alliance with the United

States puts it in a precarious position where it cannot choose between being pro-China *or* pro-Taiwan and instead must opt for an approach that combines deterrence with diplomacy.

Though much of this discussion about foreign relations has centered on what would be considered "traditional" security issues, Japan's national security policy is not limited solely to military considerations; in fact, for most of the Cold War, external security policy was anchored by economic policy, not by the military. Today, Japan engages in a "soft power" approach to diplomacy through official development assistance (ODA), the bulk of which is administered by the Japan International Cooperation Agency. Much of this ODA goes toward human security development efforts, such as projects for emergency recovery from natural disasters or public health crises, or to long-term projects like education or economic development. The SDF also engages in disaster relief efforts at home and abroad; for example, it assisted with the recovery after the Kobe earthquake and in Indonesia in 2018 after a tsunami. Japan regularly hosts high-profile international events, like the meeting of the G20 states or the Olympics in the summer of 2021. Japan also leverages extensive cultural soft power resources through the popularity of anime, manga, video games, and Japanese cuisine. If we return to our opening scene at the 2016 Olympics, Abe Shinzo in a Mario outfit exemplifies the soft power allure of the host city Tokyo vis-à-vis the hard power of other recent hosts like China or Russia.

Though much of the discussion of Japan's foreign policy inherently involves talking about the United States, Japan is a leader in its own right. Tokyo developed the Free and Open Indo-Pacific Strategy in 2016 before the United States adopted it as a policy goal in 2019. It was also Japan's idea of "values-based" foreign policy and closer ties with the democratic countries of India and Australia that revived the Quadrilateral Dialogue. Ties have since deepened between Japan and Australia as the two are now conducting joint military drills and working toward a new bilateral defense pact. Relations with India are perhaps the fastest growing in the region as Tokyo and New Delhi have increased the integration of their economies and are developing a civil nuclear deal. While China's Belt and Road investment initiative is gaining a lot of attention, Japan has invested in Southeast Asian countries' infrastructure over the course of decades through cooperation with the Association for Southeast Asian Nations (ASEAN). Tokyo has also pivoted from an aid-only approach to African development initiatives to a more holistic partnership that involves working with the private sector on sustainable development and critical infrastructure projects. While Japan can't hope to compete dollar-for-dollar with China in terms of African investments, it can place East African countries at the center of the Indo-Pacific security strategy, a move that will benefit countries in East Africa as well as Japan's long-term foreign policy goals.

Japan has repeatedly proven to be remarkably capable of adapting to change. In an era of Western colonization, Japan excelled at military expansionism. In the wake of military defeat, it built an economic empire. When the West turned against Communism, it proved itself a reliable regional ally. While Japan may not have made the rules of the international system, it has demonstrated remarkably well how to prosper under them.[4]

7

Conclusions and Looking Ahead

In past years, the world has seen the rise of populist leaders in democracies across the world, from the United States and France to Brazil and South Africa. While there is no universal definition to help us identify populism, it is often characterized by a charismatic leader who claims to identify with the people and who is struggling against corrupt elites who want to block progress. While those sentiments alone may not cause harm, leaders can capitalize on the dissatisfaction these beliefs capture to erode the trust in and legitimacy of democratic practices and institutions and to pit groups against each other in a game of division and exclusion. When leaders of any political party publicly contest the outcomes of elections by falsely claiming they were illegitimate, or when the media cannot function freely as a watchdog on government, democracy as a whole suffers. We can generally agree that populist sentiment seems to be less prevalent in Japan than in many other democratic nations at this historical moment, and as these nations struggle to contain some of the excesses of populist sentiment, this may be a good time to ask "why?" There are a few theories we can briefly explore here.

Some argue that the structure of the Japanese political system creates a barrier to populist parties or leaders gaining traction. Prime ministers don't hold the same power or mandate as independently elected presidents, and in Japan at least, they tend to lack the charisma needed to win a national election. Instead, prime ministers are elevated through the party by playing by party rules. Polls favored the outspoken nonconformist LDP House of Representatives member Taro Kono to be the LDP pick for prime minister in 2021, but the "maverick" was passed over for the safer choice, Kishida. The breakup of powerful unions in 1987 and the Socialist Party of Japan ten years later essentially limited space for anti-establishment sentiment or movements to grow. The DPJ failure in office from 2009 to 2012 also tempered enthusiasm and expectations for a real alternative to the LDP, in effect preventing the kind of polarized politics we see in the United States. Despite the regional success of Ishin no Kai, or the "Japan Innovation Party," it has so far been unable to expand its appeal as Nippon Ishin much beyond the Kansai region. Furthermore, despite often being labeled a populist opposition party, many of Ishin's policies align with those of the LDP. It is also difficult for outsiders to gain entrée into the Japanese political system. The need for koenaki support groups, party affiliation, familial lineages, or other personal ties essentially limit who can be successful in seeking office—it's not a system where you can simply "buy" your way in. Ironically, many of the features of the Japanese political system that are often criticized—predictable party politics; a weak, ineffectual opposition; and a largely inaccessible system—seem to have allowed populist sentiment to bypass Japan.

Other explanations focus outside the political system. Japan has maintained social programs and a wider social safety net more effectively than many other countries, leading to lower levels of inequality. The divide between the wealthy and everyone else is also smaller, a result of very high inheritance and income tax rates. There are, of course, wealthy people, but ostentatious displays of wealth are considered generally to be in poor taste and are socially discouraged. Though inequality has increased in Japan over the past twenty years, there is still no widespread conversation about the "1 Percent," nor is there backlash against elites that we see in the United States and elsewhere.

Perhaps part of the explanation also lies in Japan's national identity. As a nation-state, Japan's citizens are relatively homogenous in language, culture, and ethnicity, though the country does include many minority groups of ethnically distinct people, like the Ryūkyū islanders, Ainu, and ethnic Koreans. This common identity, plus the geographic and historical imperative of living on an island with limited space and few natural resources, means Japanese people are accustomed to being asked to band together for a common cause. In the months following the Fukushima Daiichi nuclear disaster of March of 2011, for example, a movement called *setsuden,* or "power-saving," swept through Japan, encouraging consumers to use less electricity while electricity-supplying nuclear reactors were going offline for safety checks. As a result, the total electricity supplied by the ten major utility companies across Japan dropped 9 percent by July 2011.

Yet it's not enough for a population to simply lack significant diversity. Any democracy that protects free speech is subject to the risk of the rise of demagogic politicians who vilify certain ethnic minorities or socioeconomic classes. For conservative people who live in rural areas, the "other" might be liberal urban-dwellers; for those who have lost their jobs to globalization, it may be people in other countries. The "other" might be immigrants who politicians warn will drain national resources. The social biases we find in every country are also present in Japan, and this volume includes some but not nearly all of the social and political challenges for minority groups living there. In 2010, UN human rights experts called out Japan for racism, discrimination, and exploitation of migrant workers. A 2017 national government survey revealed reports of employment discrimination, racist taunts, discriminatory speech, Japanese-only recruitment, and the denial of rental applications. Racism and xenophobia are not absent from government, either. In a speech in 2000, Tokyo Governor Ishihara Shintaro said that foreigners were committing terrible crimes and would cause civil disorder in the event of a national disaster, and he was reelected three times before stepping down. Even though these sentiments exist, they are rarely leveraged as political tactics meant to divide and exclude. When the Abe government streamlined the immigration process to allow entrance for more foreign workers, the policy was accompanied with a pragmatic message: regardless of personal feelings, with labor shortages and a shrinking population, immigration must be a part of the solution to Japan's *collective* demographic challenges. Perhaps the explanation lies in the LDP's continued dominance and the fact that they don't have to divide and polarize voters to win elections.

Although Japan has managed to avoid the recent trend of skepticism toward efforts to strengthen liberal democracy we find elsewhere, there are still significant political challenges Japanese must face. Interestingly, many of these challenges stem from factors already mentioned here. The weakening of major political competition to the LDP—externally from opposition parties and internally from the LDP's factions—is problematic. As transparency and accountability weaken, corruption becomes more likely. Without the threat of challenge from opposition, majority parties become less attuned to the public's demands. Opinion polls show that Japanese citizens tend to be more progressive than their government, but as long as small voting cores can still deliver majority victories, the government will continue to grow increasingly out of touch with the people. We are already seeing the results of this trend as voter turnout, especially among young people, remains low and polls show depressed levels of interest in political participation. When Abe and Koike invited the world to Japan in 2016, they did not anticipate that the COVID-19 pandemic would disrupt all levels of economic and political life, and it is still too early to try to understand all the ways it will. Compared to other countries in East Asia, Japan has been able to contain the virus without a gross neglect of civil rights and liberties. We might see an increased interest in political participation in response to the government's handling of the crisis, whether it is successful or not.

Beyond its own borders, Japan also faces significant regional and international challenges. Democratic regression and the decline of the liberal international order is a mutual concern of the United States and Japan. But the Biden administration is currently grappling with multiple national and international problems, ranging from inflation to the war in Ukraine to what is perhaps the most politically divided nation since shortly before the American Civil War. So far, Japan's "values-based" foreign policy has relied on pragmatism and utility that requires dealing with authoritarian governments rather than promoting regime change and foregoing any introspection on its own human rights record. Japan has stepped into a space perhaps created by a weakening of American leadership and should continue strengthening partnerships with countries around the world. Formal agreements now exist that are focused on free trade and creating an area of free and safe data flows between Europe and Japan. A Japanese idea, "Data Free Flow with Trust," is now a major initiative at the G20. Japan has also worked to build relationships with countries in the Middle East, pursuing what has been called "proactive pacifism" in the region—for example, acting as a mediator between the US and Iran over a nuclear deal. Japan—having emerged, unlike the US, from limited intervention in Iraq and Afghanistan with its reputation intact—is in the unique position of being a NATO ally with a history of promoting a peaceful, liberal world order that retains legitimacy in the Middle East. One of the most obvious conclusions emerging from the COVID-19 pandemic is that twenty-first-century transnational problems will require transnational collaboration. From climate change to public health, states can't go it alone. In this respect, Japan is ahead of the curve.

All forms of government justify themselves as serving best the interests of the people. In this way, a democracy is no different from a system of despotism. Compared to other forms of government, however, democracy is a relatively new experiment. British historian Sir Henry Sumner Maine said that of all forms of government, democracy is the most difficult. We can see that claim borne out empirically by observing that democratic transitions fail more often than they succeed. Japan, a non-Western country where this transition was successful, has been called "an uncommon democracy." In some ways, that is true, and this book has explored where Japanese democracy departs from practices in other places. Yet the most significant thing democracy in Japan has in common with other places is that it is imperfect. Joseph Dana Miller wrote in 1915 that those who are disappointed with the results of democracy should remember that infants fall many times before they are able to walk; so, too, will democracies stumble, leaning on rotten pillars or regressing to a crawl before they can walk independently. Maybe, then, the cure for democracy is not more democracy but rather more knowledge—of ourselves, and of each other.

NOTES

INTRODUCTION

[1] Prime Minister Abe Shinzo retired from the position of prime minister in September of 2020. He was assassinated in July of 2022.

CHAPTER 1

[1] "Confucian Teaching: The Emperor and the Mandate of Heaven," *Asia for Educators*, Columbia University, accessed June 1, 2022., http://afe.easia.columbia.edu/at/conf_teaching/ct13.html.

[2] See John Dower, "Black Ships and Samurai: Commodore Perry and the Opening of Japan (1853–1854)," MIT's Visualizing Cultures, 2010, accessed September 13, 2020, http://visualizingcultures.mit.edu/black_ships_and_samurai/index.html.

[3] See Stephen Vlastos, *Peasant Protests and Uprisings in Tokugawa Japan* (Berkeley: University of California Press, 1990).

[4] James Huffman, *Modern Japan: A History in Documents* (Oxford: Oxford University Press, 2010), 39.

[5] *Asia for Educators*, Columbia University, 2022, accessed October 3, 2020, http://afe.easia.columbia.edu.

[6] Thomas Donald Conlan, *From Sovereign to Symbol: An Age of Ritual Determinism in Fourteenth-Century Japan* (Oxford: Oxford University Press, 2011), 70–77.

[7] Angus Maddison, *Contours of the World Economy, 1–2030 AD: Essays in Macro-Economic History* (Oxford: Oxford University Press, 2007).

[8] "Modern Japan and France: Adoration, Encounter, and Interaction," National Diet Library of Japan, 2014, accessed October 15, 2020, https://www.ndl.go.jp/france/en/part1/s1_2.html.

[9] Hirobumi Itō. *Commentaries on the Constitution of the Empire of Japan* (Hardpress, 2012).

[10] "Taisho Democracy in Japan: 1912–1926." *Facing History*, accessed October 15, 2020, https://www.facinghistory.org/nanjing-atrocities/nation-building/taisho-democracy-japan-1912-1926.

[11] David Kenley, *Modern Chinese History*, 2nd edition (Ann Arbor: Association for Asian Studies, 2020), 52.

[12] Bret Fisk and Cary Karacas, "The Firebombing of Tokyo and Its Legacy: An Introduction," *Asia-Pacific Journal* 9, no. 3 (2011), https://apjjf.org/2011/9/3/Bret-Fisk/3469/article.html.

[13] See John Dower's *Embracing Defeat: Japan in the Wake of World War II* (New York: W. W. Norton, 2000) for a comprehensive look at the Allied Occupation period in Japan.

CHAPTER 2

[1] "MacArthur Notes (MacArthur's Three Basic Points, February 3, 1946," *Birth of the Constitution of Japan*, National Diet Library, 2003–2004, accessed September 23, 2020, https://www.ndl.go.jp/constitution/e/shiryo/03/072shoshi.html.

[2] Japan: Interpretations of Article 9 of the Constitution, Law Library of Congress (U.S.). Global Legal Research Directorate, 2015, accessed 14 September 2022. https://hdl.loc.gov/loc.law/llglrd.2016295698.

[3] "Constitutional Change in Japan: Japan's Postwar Constitution," Council on Foreign Relations, accessed October 18, 2020, https://www.cfr.org/japan-constitution/japans-postwar-constitution.

[4] Shinohara Hajime, "Postwar Parties and Politics in Japan," *Developing Economies* 6, no. 4 (December 1968).

[5] "United Nations Charter (full text)," United Nations, accessed October 20, 2020, https://www.un.org/en/sections/un-charter/un-charter-full-text/.

[6] Reiji Yoshida, "The Realist behind the Idealist Constitution," *Japan Times*, August 17, 2014.

[7] Lindsay Maizland and Beina Xu, "The US-Japan Security Alliance," Council on Foreign Relations, 2021, accessed October 15, 2020, https://www.cfr.org/backgrounder/us-japan-security-alliance.

[8] Justin Jesty, "Tokyo 1960: Days of Rage and Grief," MIT Visualizing Cultures, 2012, accessed September 20, 2020, https://visualizingcultures.mit.edu/tokyo_1960/anp2_essay01.html.

[9] "Constitutional Change in Japan: The Politics of Revision," Council on Foreign Relations, 2022, accessed October 15, 2020, https://www.cfr.org/japan-constitution/politics-of-revision.

[10] Dalin Hamilton, "Will Abe's Constitutional Concessions Be Enough?" *East Asia Forum* (March 8, 2018), https://www.eastasiaforum.org/2018/03/08/will-abes-constitutional-concessions-be-enough.

CHAPTER 3

[1] George R. Packard, "Democracy in Japan: Why Should Americans Care?" *Education about Asia* 16, no. 1 (Spring 2011).

[2] Norimitsu Onishi, "Japan Learns Dreaded Task of Jury Duty," *New York Times,* July 16, 2007.

[3] David S. Law, "Why Has Judicial Review Failed in Japan?" *Washington University Law Review* 88, no. 6 (2011).

[4] Joji Watanuki, "Social Structure and Voting Behavior," in *The Japanese Voter*, edited by Scott C. Flanagan, Shinsaku Kohei, Ichiro Miyake, Bradley M. Richardson, and Joji Watanuki (New Haven: Yale University Press, 1991), 49–83.

[5] Purnendra Jain, "Japan's Pivotal Local Elections will Impact National Politics," *East Asia Forum*, April 4, 2019, https://www.eastasiaforum.org/2019/04/04/japans-pivotal-local-elections-will-impact-national-politics/.

[6] Institute for Democracy and Electoral Assistance country profile data: Japan, accessed February 13, 2021, https://www.idea.int/data-tools/country-view/155/40.

[7] Masaru Kohno, "Voter Turnout and Strategic Ticket-Splitting under Japan's New Electoral Rules," *Asian Survey* 37, no. 5 (May 1997).

[8] Miho Nakatani, "What Happened when Japan Lowered the Minimum Voting Age?" *East Asia Forum*, October 21, 2017, https://www.eastasiaforum.org/2017/10/21/what-happened-when-japan-lowered-the-minimum-voting-age/.

[9] Purnendra Jain and Takeshi Kobayashi, "Political Dynasties Dominate Japan's Democracy," *East Asia Forum*, March 13, 2018, https://www.eastasiaforum.org/2018/03/13/political-dynasties-dominate-japans-democracy/.

[10] The Triple Disaster refers to the earthquake, tsunami, and nuclear disaster of 2011.

CHAPTER 4

[1] See Max Weber, *The Protestant Ethic and the Spirit of Capitalism* (London: George Allen and Unwin, 1930).

[2] Chalmers Johnson, *MITI and the Japanese Miracle: The Growth of Industrial Policy, 1925–1975.*

[3] John M. Maki, "The Role of Bureaucracy in Japan," *Pacific Affairs* 20, no. 4 (Dec 1947), 391–406.

[4] In 2001, MITI merged with other agencies during the Central Government Reform to become the Ministry of Economy, Trade, and Industry (METI).

[5] Jeffrey Alexander, "Honda Soichiro and the Rise of Japan's Postwar Motor Vehicle Industry," *Education About Asia* 20, no. 2 (Fall 2015).

[6] Zhiqun Zhu. *Understanding East Asia's Economic 'Miracles'* (Ann Arbor: Association for Asian Studies, 2016).

[7] B. C. Koh, "The Recruitment of Higher Civil Servants in Japan: A Comparative Perspective," *Asian Survey* 25, no. 3 (March 1985), 292–309.

[8] "Government and Politics in Japan," *Asia for Educators*, Columbia University, accessed June 30, 2021, http://afe.easia.columbia.edu/special/japan_1950_politics.htm#bur.

[9] "Women Set Record 25.8% Pass Rate on Civil Service Exam," *Japan Times*, June 30, 2017, https://www.japantimes.co.jp/news/2017/06/30/national/women-set-record-25-8-pass-rate-civil-service-exam.

CHAPTER 5

[1] Robert Pekkanen, "Grass Roots Democracy and Civil Society in East Asia," *Education About Asia* 16, no. 3 (Winter 2011).

[2] There is some debate as to whether labor unions and business organizations are part of civil society.

[3] For a discussion of "bridging" and "bonding" social capital, see Robert Putnam's *Bowling Alone* (New York: Simon & Schuster, 2000).

[4] Tsujinaka, Yutaka. "Civil Society and Social Capital in Japan," in *International Encyclopedia of Civil Society*, edited by Helmut K. Anheier and Stefan Toepler (Springer: Springer Science and Business Media, 2010).

[5] Hirata Keiko, *Civil Society in Japan: The Growing Role of NGOs in Tokyo's Aid and Development Policy* (Springer: Springer Science and Business Media, 2002).

[6] Tsujinaka, Yutaka, "Civil Society and Social Capital in Japan."

[7] Ralph J. D. Braibanti, "Neighborhood Association in Japan and their Democratic Potentialities," *Far Eastern Quarterly* 7, no. 2 (Feb. 1948): 136–174.

[8] Japan Ministry on Health, Labor, and Welfare, White Paper on Health, Labor, and Welfare—Thinking about a Declining Population, accessed October 18, 2021. https://www.mhlw.go.jp/wp/hakusyo/kousei/15/backdata/01-01-03-115.html.

CHAPTER 6

[1] Prime ministers cannot have served in the Self-Defense Forces prior to entering office.

[2] Lowy Institute's Asia Power Index, 2021 Edition: Japan, https://power.lowyinstitute.org/countries/japan.

[3] TPP negotiations list an unwillingness to lower subsidies for state enterprise as a main reason for China's exclusion from an organization meant to promote free trade.

[4] Richard D. Leitch, Akira Kato, and Martin E. Weinstein, *Japan's Role in the Post-Cold World*, (Westport: Greenwood Press, 1995), 6.

GLOSSARY

Amakudari: a practice in which senior bureaucrats retire to elite positions in public and private sectors.

Bakufu: another word for shogunate, bakufu means "tent government," referring to a government administered by a military commander (a shogun, in this case) from the field of battle, perhaps while under a tent. This term refers to the shogun's government in power during the Edo period.

Bureaucracy: civil servants acting together as an administrative arm of the state.

Checkbook diplomacy: foreign policy that prefers donating monetary aid rather than direct military intervention.

Civil society: Distinct from government and business, civil society is the network of citizens joined by common interests and activities in a society.

Consolidated democracy: a system where aspects of democracy—like free and fair elections, the full recognition of civil liberties, the rule of law, and a free press—are institutionalized to the extent that they are relatively invulnerable to outside shocks. In other words, consolidated democracies are mature and strong democracies compared to transitioning or weakening democracies.

Daimyō: feudal lords during the Edo period who possessed vast holdings of land.

The Diet: the English term for the Japanese national governing body. A term borrowed from Prussian and reflective of European influence on the structure of the Japanese national legislature.

Fukoku Kyōhei: the slogan of the Japanese military during the early Meiji era, meaning "rich country, strong army."

Genrō: a small group of retired, elder statesmen who acted as informal advisers to the emperor and to key government officials. The last surviving genrō, Kinmochi Saionji, was one of the most influential voices in politics throughout the 1920s and 1930s. The institution of the genrō died with Kinmochi in 1940.

Gunboat diplomacy: the pursuit of foreign policy objectives with the conspicuous use of naval power.

House of Councillors: the smaller, upper governing body in Japan's bicameral parliamentary legislature.

House of Representatives: the larger, more powerful lower governing body in Japan's bicameral parliamentary legislature.

Keiretsu: a conglomeration of businesses linked together by cross holdings of shares.

Kisha **club**: a news gathering association of reporters from various news organization outlets.

Koenkai: local support groups for political candidates and politicians.

Meiji era: a period between 1868 and 1912 under the leadership of Emperor Mutsuhito, or Meiji, meaning "enlightened rule." The Meiji era was a period characterized by industrialization, modernization, and, to some degree, Westernization.

Ministry of Economy, Trade, and Industry (METI): bureaucracy created by the 2001 Central Governmental Reform. METI has a wide mandate, covering, among other things, areas such as trade and industry, energy security and regulation, and arms exports.

Ministry of Finance: Government body in charge of public finance and monetary affairs.

Ministry of International Trade and Industry (MITI): bureaucracy that guided many economic policy decisions, for better or worse, from the 1950s to the 1980s. In 2001, MITI merged with other agencies to form the Ministry of Economy, Trade, and Industry (METI).

Multimember district: an electoral district that holds elections where multiple seats are available and votes are allocated with single nontransferrable voting.

Neighborhood associations: Local groups that coordinate community activities.

Nemawashi: the translation of nemawashi is close to "digging around the roots." We can understand nemawashi as decision-making by consensus when big changes are being proposed.

Organization for Economic Cooperation and Development: international organization in which members describe themselves as being dedicated to democracy and a market economy and to working together to find shared solutions for common problems.

Pax Tokugawa: the "Tokugawa Peace," or a period from the seventeenth to the nineteenth centuries characterized by relative domestic peace.

Rule of law: the mechanisms, processes, institutions, practices, or norms that support the equality of all citizens before the law, secure a nonarbitrary form of government, and more generally prevent the arbitrary use of power.

Saiban-in: A judicial system in which people from the public are selected to participate as lay judges in criminal trials.

Sakoku: a "chained" or "locked" country. Sakoku refers to Tokugawa policies of the 1630s that limited the movement of people and goods in and out of Japan.

Single-member district: a district that holds elections where one candidate, the candidate with the most votes, will win the open seat.

Single nontransferrable voting: a system of plurality where the candidate with the most votes gets the open seat. When used in multimember districts, the seats will be awarded according to most votes, second-most votes, etc.

Shōwa era: a period from 1926 to 1989 under the leadership of Emperor Hirohito, or Shōwa. The early years of the Shōwa era were characterized by ultranationalism and militarism. Following the end of World War II, the Shōwa era brought periods of democratization and economic growth.

Sovereignty: the authority of a state to govern itself. In democracies, we commonly say that sovereignty rests with the people rather than with a monarch or single authoritarian figure.

Taishō era: a period from 1912 to 1926 under the leadership of Emperor Yoshihito, or Taishō. Because Emperor Taishō was frequently ill, power shifted from the genrō to the Imperial Diet during this time. The Taishō period is often called a brief period of liberalism, or Taishō democracy, between the preceding Meiji era and the following Shōwa era.

Treaty of Kanagawa: also known as the US-Japan Treaty of Peace and Amity, the 1854 treaty allowed for the establishment of a US consulate in Shimoda and safe passage for shipwrecked American sailors. It also opened Japanese ports at Shimoda and Hakodate (among other things).

Zaibatsu: industrial and financially vertically integrated private parent companies with subsidiaries that enjoyed oligopolistic positions in the early twentieth century. Mitsubishi, for example, is one of five such companies that controlled much of Japanese industry and trade leading up to World War II.

BIBLIOGRAPHY

Alexander, Jeffrey. "Honda Soichiro and the Rise of Japan's Postwar Motor Vehicle Industry." *Education About Asia* 20, no. 2 (Fall 2015), https://www.asianstudies.org/publications/eaa/archives/honda-soichiro-and-the-rise-of-japans-postwar-motor-vehicle-industry.

Braibanti, Ralph J. D. "Neighborhood Association in Japan and their Democratic Potentialities." *Far Eastern Quarterly* 7, no. 2 (Feb 1948).

"Confucian Teaching: The Emperor and the Mandate of Heaven." *Asia for Educators*, Columbia University. Accessed June 1, 2022, http://afe.easia.columbia.edu/at/conf_teaching/ct13.html.

Conlan, Thomas Donald. *From Sovereign to Symbol: An Age of Ritual Determinism in Fourteenth-Century Japan.* Oxford: Oxford University Press, 2011.

Council on Foreign Relations. "Constitutional Change in Japan: Japan's Postwar Constitution." Accessed October 18, 2020, https://www.cfr.org/japan-constitution/japans-postwar-constitution.

Council on Foreign Relations. "Constitutional Change in Japan: The Politics of Revision." Accessed October 15, 2020, https://www.cfr.org/japan-constitution/politics-of-revision.

Curtis, Gerald L. *The Japanese Way of Politics.* New York: Columbia University Press, 1988.

Dower, John. "Black Ships and Samurai: Commodore Perry and the Opening of Japan (1853–1854)." MIT's Visualizing Cultures. Accessed September 13, 2020, http://visualizingcultures.mit.edu/black_ships_and_samurai/index.html.

———. *Embracing Defeat: Japan in the Wake of World War II.* New York: W. W. Norton & Company, 1999.

Fisk, Bret and Cary Karacas. "The Firebombing of Tokyo and Its Legacy: An Introduction." *Asia Pacific Journal: Japan Focus* 9, no. 3 (2011), https://apjjf.org/2011/9/3/Bret-Fisk/3469/article.html.

Funabashi, Yoichi and Koichi Nakano, editors. *The Democratic Party of Japan in Power: Challenges and Failures.* Translated by Kate Dunlop. New York: Routledge, 2017.

"Government and Politics in Japan," *Asia for Educators*, Columbia University. Accessed June 30, 2021, http://afe.easia.columbia.edu/special/japan_1950_politics.htm#bur.

Hajime, Shinohara. "Postwar Parties and Politics in Japan." *The Developing Economies* 6, no. 4 (December 1968).

Hamilton, Dalin. "Will Abe's Constitutional Concessions Be Enough?" *East Asia Forum*. March 8, 2018, https://www.eastasiaforum.org/2018/03/08/will-abes-constitutional-concessions-be-enough/.

Harris, Tobias S. *The Iconoclast: Shinzō Abe and the New Japan*. London: Hurst & Company, 2020

Hayes, Louis D. *Introduction to Japanese Politics*. 5th edition. New York: M. E. Sharpe Inc., 2009.

Hirata, Keiko, *Civil Society in Japan: The Growing Role of NGOs in Tokyo's Aid and Development Policy*. Springer: Springer Science and Business Media, 2002.

Huffman, James. *Modern Japan: A History in Documents*. Oxford: Oxford University Press, 2010.

Institute for Democracy and Electoral Assistance country profile data: Japan. Accessed February 13, 2021, https://www.idea.int/data-tools/country-view/155/40.

Itō, Hirobumi. *Commentaries on the Constitution of the Empire of Japan*. Hardpress, 2012.Jain, Purnendra. "Japan's Pivotal Local Elections Will Impact National Politics." *East Asia Forum*, April 4, 2019, https://www.eastasiaforum.org/2019/04/04/japans-pivotal-local-elections-will-impact-national-politics.

Jain, Purnendra and Takeshi Kobayashi. "Political Dynasties Dominate Japan's Democracy." *East Asia Forum*. March 13, 2018, https://www.eastasiaforum.org/2018/03/13/political-dynasties-dominate-japans-democracy.

Jamitsky, Ulli. "The TPP Debate in Japan: Reasons for a Failed Protest Campaign." *Asia Pacific Perspectives 13*. (Spring/Summer 2015).

Japan: Interpretations of Article 9 of the Constitution, Law Library of Congress (U.S.). Global Legal Research Directorate, 2015. Accessed 14 September 2022. https://hdl.loc.gov/loc.law/llglrd.2016295698, https://www.loc.gov/law/help/japan-constitution/interpretations-article9.php#Pacifist.

Japan Ministry of Health, Labor, and Welfare. 2015 White Paper on Health, Labor, and Welfare—Thinking about a Declining Population. Accessed October 18, 2021, https://www.mhlw.go.jp/wp/hakusyo/kousei/15/backdata/01-01-03-115.html.

Jesty, Justin. "Tokyo 1960: Days of Rage and Grief." MIT Visualizing Cultures. Accessed September 20, 2020, https://visualizingcultures.mit.edu/tokyo_1960/anp2_essay01.html.

Johnson, Chalmers. *MITI and the Japanese Miracle: The Growth of Industrial Policy, 1925–1975*. Stanford: Stanford University Press, 1982.

Kenley, David. *Modern Chinese History*. 2nd edition. Ann Arbor: Association for Asian Studies, 2020.

Kingston, Jeffrey. "The Emptiness of Japan's Values Diplomacy in Asia." *The Asia-Pacific Journal: Japan Focus*. Vol 18: 19: 1, 1 October 2020.

Kitaoka, Shinichi. *The Political History of Modern Japan*. Translated by Robert D. Eldridge with Graham Leonard. Routledge. London and New York: Routledge, 2018.

Koh, B. C. "The Recruitment of Higher Civil Servants in Japan: A Comparative Perspective." *Asian Survey* 25, no. 3 (March 1985).

Kohno, Masaru. "Voter Turnout and Strategic Ticket-Splitting under Japan's New Electoral Rules." *Asian Survey* 37 no. 5 (May 1997).

Krauss, Ellis S. and Robert J. Pekkanen. *The Rise and Fall of Japan's LDP: Political Party Organizations as Historical Institutions*. Ithaca and London: Cornell University Press, 2011.

Law, David S. "Why Has Judicial Review Failed in Japan?" *Washington University Law Review* 88, no. 6 (2011).

Leitch, Richard D. Akira Kato and Martin E. Weinstein, Japan's Role in the Post-Cold World. Westport, CT: Greenwood Press, 1995.

Lowy Institute's Asia Power Index, 2021 Edition: Japan, https://power.lowyinstitute.org/countries/japan.

"MacArthur Notes (MacArthur's Three Basic Points, February 3, 1946." *Birth of the Constitution of Japan*. National Diet Library. Accessed September 23, 2020, https://www.ndl.go.jp/constitution/e/shiryo/03/072shoshi.html.

Maddison, Angus. *Contours of the World Economy, 1–2030 AD: Essays in Macro-Economic History*. Oxford: Oxford University Press, 2007.

Maizland, Lindsay and Beina Xu. "The US-Japan Security Alliance." Council on Foreign Relations. Accessed October 15, 2020, https://www.cfr.org/backgrounder/us-japan-security-alliance.

Maki, John M. "The Role of Bureaucracy in Japan." *Pacific Affairs* 20, no. 4 (Dec 1947).

"Modern Japan and France: Adoration, Encounter, and Interaction." National Diet Library of Japan. Accessed October 15, 2020, https://www.ndl.go.jp/france/en/part1/s1_2.html.

Nakatani, Miho. "What Happened when Japan Lowered the Minimum Voting Age?" *East Asia Forum*. October 21, 2017, https://www.eastasiaforum.org/2017/10/21/what-happened-when-japan-lowered-the-minimum-voting-age.

Onishi, Norimitsu. "Japan Learns Dreaded Task of Jury Duty." *New York Times,* July 16, 2007.

Packard, George R. "Democracy in Japan: Why Should Americans Care?" *Education about Asia* 16, no. 1 (Spring 2011).

Pekkanen, Robert. "Grass Roots Democracy and Civil Society in East Asia." *Education about Asia* 16, no. 3 (Winter 2011).

Pempel, T. J., ed. *Uncommon Democracies: The One-Party Dominant Regimes.* Ithaca and London: Cornell University Press, 1990.

Putnam, Robert. *Bowling Alone.* New York: Simon & Schuster, 2000.

"Taisho Democracy in Japan: 1912–1926." *Facing History.* Accessed October 15, 2020, https://www.facinghistory.org/nanjing-atrocities/nation-building/taisho-democracy-japan-1912-1926.

Takii, Kazuhiro. *The Meiji Constitution: The Japanese Experience of the West and the Shaping of the Modern State.* Japan: International House of Japan, 2007.

Tsujinaka, Yutaka. "Civil Society and Social Capital in Japan." In *International Encyclopedia of Civil Society*, edited by Helmut K. Anheier and Stefan Toepler. Springer: Springer Publishing, 2010.

United Nations. "United Nations Charter (full text)." Accessed on October 20, 2020, https://www.un.org/en/sections/un-charter/un-charter-full-text.

Vlastos, Stephen. *Peasant Protests and Uprisings in Tokugawa Japan.* Berkeley: University of California Press, 1990.

Watanuki, Joji. "Social Structure and Voting Behavior." In *The Japanese Voter*, edited by Scott C. Flanagan, Shinsaku Kohei, Ichiro Miyake, Bradley M. Richardson, and Joji Watanuki. New Haven: Yale University Press, 1991.

Weber, Max. *The Protestant Ethic and the Spirit of Capitalism.* London: George Allen and Unwin, 1930.

"Women Set Record 25.8% Pass Rate on Civil Service Exam." *Japan Times.* June 30, 2017, https://www.japantimes.co.jp/news/2017/06/30/national/women-set-record-25-8-pass-rate-civil-service-exam.

Yoshida, Reiji. "The Realist Behind the Idealist Constitution." *Japan Times*. August 17, 2014.

Zhu, Zhiqun. *Understanding East Asia's Economic 'Miracles.'* Ann Arbor: Association for Asian Studies, 2016.

Resources for Further Study

Pre-Meiji Politics

Burkman, Thomas. "Democracy in Japan: Foreign Stimuli and Domestic Leadership." *Education About Asia* 16, no. 1 (Spring 2011).

Conlan, Thomas Donald. *From Sovereign to Symbol: An Age of Ritual Determinism in Fourteenth-Century Japan.* Oxford: Oxford University Press, 2011.

Hall, John Whitney, et al. *Japan Before Tokugawa: Political Consolidation and Economic Growth, 1500–1650.* Princeton: Princeton University Press, 1981.

Kang, David C. *East Asia before the West: Five Centuries of Trade and Tribute.* New York: Columbia University Press, 2010.

Roberts, Luke S. *Performing the Great Peace: Political Space and Open Secrets in Tokugawa Japan.* Honolulu: University of Hawai'i Press, 2012.

Vlastos, Stephen. *Peasant Protests and Uprisings in Tokugawa Japan.* Berkeley: University of California Press, 1986.

Meiji Era Politics

Itō, Hirobumi. *Commentaries on the Constitution of the Empire of Japan* (Hardpress, 2012).

Métraux, Daniel. "Democratic Trends in Meiji Japan." *Education About Asia* 16, no. 1 (Spring 2011).

Ramseyer, J. Mark and Frances M. Rosenbluth. *The Politics of Oligarchy: Institutional Choice in Meiji Japan.* Cambridge: Cambridge University Press, 1998.

Takii, Kazuhiro. *Ito Hirobumi: Japan's First Prime Minister and Father of the Meiji Constitution.* New York: Routledge, 2016.

Takii, Kazuhiro. *The Meiji Constitution: The Japanese Experience of the West and the Shaping of the Modern State.* Japan: International House of Japan, 2007.

Walthall, Anne and M. William Steele. *Politics and Society in Japan's Meiji Restoration.* New York: Bedford/St. Martin's Press, 2016.

World War II and Occupation-Era Politics

Dower, John. *Embracing Defeat: Japan in the Wake of World War II*. New York: W. W. Norton & Company, 1999.

Eisman, Ron and John Frank. "Japan 1945: A US Marine's Photographs from Ground Zero." Five Colleges Center for East Asian Studies, September 20, 2018, Webinar.

Fisk, Bret and Cary Karacas. "The Firebombing of Tokyo and Its Legacy: An Introduction." *Asia-Pacific Journal* 9, no. 3: 2017, https://apjjf.org/2011/9/3/Bret-Fisk/3469/article.html.

Shillony, Ben-Ami. *Politics and Culture in Wartime Japan*. Oxford: Oxford University Press, 1991.

Toland, John. *The Rising Sun: The Decline and Fall of the Japanese Empire, 1936–1945*. New York: Modern Library, 2003.

Post-World War Two Politics

Curtis, Gerald. *Election Campaigning Japanese Style*. New York: Columbia University Press, 1971.

———. *The Japanese Way of Politics* (New York: Columbia University Press, 1988).

———. *The Logic of Japanese Politics*. New York: Columbia University Press, 1999.

Dower, John. *Ways of Remembering, Ways of Forgetting: Japan in the Modern World*. New York: New Press, 2012.

------ *The Logic of Japanese Politics*. Columbia University Press, 1999.

Dunscomb, Paul E. "The Reign of Emperor Akihito, 1989–2019: A History in Five Key Words." *Education About Asia* 23, no. 3 (Winter 2018).

Elderidge, Robert D. "Japanese Millennials and Politics: An Introduction." *Education About Asia* 23, no. 1 (Spring 2018).

Funabashi, Yoichi and Koichi Nakano, editors. *The Democratic Party of Japan in Power: Challenges and Failures*. Translated by Kate Dunlop. New York: Routledge, 2017.

Fuqua, Jacques. "The Cost of Peace: Okinawa's Post-WWII History." Five Colleges Center for East Asian Studies, March 21, 2016. Webinar.

Harris, Tobias. *The Iconoclast: Shinzo Abe and the New Japan*. London: Hurst, 2020.

Hayes, Louis D. *Introduction to Japanese Politics*. 5th edition. New York: M. E. Sharpe Inc., 2009.

Hirata, K. *Civil Society in Japan: The Growing Role of NGOs in Tokyo's Aid and Development Policy*. London: Palgrave Macmillan, 2002.

Huffman, James. *Modern Japan: A History in Documents*. New York: Oxford University Press, 2004.

Inoguchi, Takahashi. *Japanese Politics: An Introduction*. Melbourne: Trans Pacific Press, 2005.

Jamitsky, Ulli. "The TPP Debate in Japan: Reasons for a Failed Protest Campaign." *Asia Pacific Perspectives* 13 (Spring/Summer 2015).

Kingston, Jeff. *Contemporary Japan: History, Politics, and Social Change Since the 1980s* Hoboken: Wiley and Sons, Inc., 2010.

Kingston, Jeff. "The Emptiness of Japan's Values Diplomacy in Asia." *Asia-Pacific Journal: Japan Focus* 18–19, no. 1 (October 2020)

———. *The Politics of Religion, Nationalism, and Identity in Asia*. Lanham: Rowman and Littlefield, 2019.

Kitaoka, Shinichi. *The Political History of Modern Japan*. Translated by Robert D. Eldridge with Graham Leonard. London and New York: Routledge, 2018.

Krauss, Ellis S and Robert J. Pekkanen. *The Rise and Fall of Japan's LDP: Political Party Organizations as Historical Institutions*. Ithaca: Cornell University Press, 2010.

Le, Tom Phuong. *Japan's Aging Peace: Pacifism and Militarism in the 21st Century*. New York: Columbia University Press, 2021.

Lind, Jennifer. *Sorry States: Apologies in International Politics*. Ithaca: Cornell University Press, 2010.

McKee, Lauren. "Sake, Sushi, and Soft Power." Five Colleges Center for East Asian Studies, February 28, 2017, Webinar.

Najita, Tetsuo. *The Intellectual Foundations of Modern Japanese Politics*. Chicago: University of Chicago Press, 1980.

Neary, Ian. *The State and Politics in Japan*, 2nd edition. Cambridge: Polity Press, 2019.

Pekkanen, Robert with Yutaka Tsujinaka and Hidehiro Yamamoto. *Neighborhood Associations and Local Governance in Japan*. London: Routledge, 2014.

Pekkanen, Robert et al (eds). *Japan Decides: 2017*. London: Palgrave Macmillan, 2018.

Pekkanen, Robert, Steven R. Reed, Daniel M. Smith (eds). *Japan Decides: 2021.* New York: Springer International Publishing, 2022.

Pempel, T. J., ed. *Uncommon Democracies: The One-Party Dominant Regimes.* Ithaca: Cornell University Press, 1990.

Pharr, Susan J. and Schwartz F. J. *The State of Civil Society in Japan.* New York: Cambridge University Press, 2003.

Reischauer, Edwin O. and Marius B. Jansen. *The Japanese Today: Change and Continuity.* Boston: Belknap Press, 1995.

Richey, Jeffrey. *Confucius in East* Asia. Ann Arbor: Association for Asian Studies, 2013.

Shinoda, Tomohito. *Koizumi Diplomacy: Japan's Kantei Approach to Diplomacy and Foreign Affairs.* Seattle: University of Washington Press, 2007.

Smith, Daniel. *Dynasties and Democracy: The Inherited Incumbency Advantage in Japan.* Redwood City: Stanford University Press, 2018.

Smith, Sheila. *Japan Rearmed: The Politics of Military Power.* Harvard University Press, 2019.

Soda, Kazuhiro, director. *Senkyo (Campaign).* Laboratory X Inc, 2007. 120 minutes.

Steel, Gill, ed. *Beyond the Gender Gap in Japan.* Ann Arbor: Michigan University Press, 2019.

Weathers, Charles. "Reformer or Destroyer? Hashimoto Toru and Populist Neoliberal Politics in Japan." *Social Science Japan Journal* 17, no. 1 (Winter 2014), 77–96.

Milton Keynes UK
Ingram Content Group UK Ltd.
UKHW010613121223
434223UK00005B/277